ROUNDING THIRD and HEADING for HOME

Praise for
ROUNDING THIRD and HEADING for HOME

"Of course, you've heard the expression that hindsight is 20/20. Sometimes it is in looking back that we get our clearest insights about what's important in life and in business. In *Rounding Third and Heading for Home*, Jay Myers uses the clarity of experience to guide us through his insights into the things that matter the most. An insightful and enjoyable look at growing a business, running a successful business, and then, ultimately, letting it go."

—Robert B. (Rob) Carter
Executive Vice President and CIO, FedEx Corporation

"From selling sodas at Tiger games as a freshman in high school in Liberty Bowl Memorial Stadium to starting his own company, Interactive Solutions, and then selling it more than twenty years later, University of Memphis alum Jay Myers has been through it all. His book helps educate other small business owners and entrepreneurs about the merger and acquisitions process, whether they choose to sell their business or not.

"As the executive in residence at the University of Memphis Fogelman College of Business & Economics, Jay has been a mentor for many U of M student entrepreneurs, including those who have started an artisan coffee shop and a logistics company. Jay offers insightful lessons, including the importance of mentors and reinventing your business before it's too late. It's great to see Jay share his hard-earned and impactful wisdom with a broader audience."

—Dr. M. David Rudd
President, University of Memphis

"*Rounding Third and Heading for Home* is a smooth at-bat for Jay. Dig into the batter's box of life and don't let the curve ball fool you.

Instead, wait on it and be ready. Smack it out of the park and enjoy that trip around the business base paths. It's another Jay Myers winner!"

—**Roy Berger**

Author, *The Most Wonderful Week of the Year* and *Big League Dream*

"I am elated that Jay Myers wrote this book. Numbers do not drive successful entrepreneurs, emotions do. This honest account of one such entrepreneur's emotional journey from seed to harvest should be required reading for anyone thinking about starting a business, running a business, or transitioning one. Prepare to be comforted and inspired. Game well played, Mr. Myers!"

—**David S. Waddell**

President, CEO Waddell & Associates, LLC

"There are the mechanics of selling a business, which should easily be handled if you surround yourself with the right advisory team. What Jay has done in this book, however, is to eloquently expose the Achilles heel in most M&A transactions: the emotional readiness of an owner to walk away from 'your baby.' Selling a business takes time and preparation around the fundamentals, but it also requires that you have honest, soul-searching conversations with yourself about walking away, handing over the reins, and what life after your business really looks like.

"Jay has done business owners a tremendous service by uncovering the emotional considerations of selling a business."

—**Domenic Rinaldi**

CBI Managing Partner, Sun Acquisitions

"Drawing upon firsthand experiences, Jay takes us along on a compelling journey of building and selling a very successful business. This is a handbook for entrepreneurs at all stages of business development."

—**Madan Birla**

Author, *FedEx Delivers* and *Unleashing Creativity and Innovation*

ROUNDING THIRD *and* HEADING *for* HOME

The Emotional Journey of Selling My Business
and the Lessons Learned Along the Way

JAY MYERS

NEW YORK

LONDON • NASHVILLE • MELBOURNE • VANCOUVER

ROUNDING THIRD and HEADING for HOME
The Emotional Journey of Selling My Business and the Lessons Learned Along the Way

© 2022 **JAY MYERS**

Published in New York, New York, by Morgan James Publishing. Morgan James is a trademark of Morgan James, LLC. www.MorganJamesPublishing.com

Proudly distributed by Ingram Publisher Services.

Morgan James BOGO™

A **FREE** ebook edition is available for you or a friend with the purchase of this print book.

CLEARLY SIGN YOUR NAME ABOVE

Instructions to claim your free ebook edition:
1. Visit MorganJamesBOGO.com
2. Sign your name CLEARLY in the space above
3. Complete the form and submit a photo of this entire page
4. You or your friend can download the ebook to your preferred device

ISBN 9781631952784 paperback
ISBN 9781631952791 eBook
Library of Congress Control Number: 2020916359

Cover Design by:
Rachel Lopez
www.r2cdesign.com

Interior Design by:
Bonnie Bushman
The Whole Caboodle Graphic Design

Morgan James PUBLISHING
Builds with... **Habitat for Humanity®** Peninsula and Greater Williamsburg

Morgan James is a proud partner of Habitat for Humanity Peninsula and Greater Williamsburg. Partners in building since 2006.

Get involved today! Visit MorganJamesPublishing.com/giving-back

To my late sister Dolores,
who was a constant source of support and
encouragement on my entrepreneurial journey

Table of Contents

Introduction: Letting My Baby Go   xi

Chapter 1   Don't Take Your Eye Off the Ball   1
Chapter 2   Not Born on Third Base   11
Chapter 3   We All Need a Mentor   21
Chapter 4   Knowing Your Brand   33
Chapter 5: The Art and Science of Professional Selling   41
Chapter 6   Don't Burn Bridges   53
Chapter 7   Employee Loyalty and Company Culture   63
Chapter 8   Reinventing Your Business Before It's Too Late   73
Chapter 9   Customer Service Can Make or Break Your Business   85
Chapter 10 Passing the Torch   97
Chapter 11 Confronting Myself: The Emotional Rollercoaster   111
            of Letting My Other Baby Go
Chapter 12 Don't Cry Because It's Over; Smile Because   131
            It Happened

Afterword   143
Acknowledgments   149
About the Author   153
Book Jay to Speak   155
Endnotes   157

Introduction: Letting My Baby Go

October 27, 2018

Savannah, Georgia

It was the perfect day for a wedding—clear skies with a slight hint of fall in the air. A year's worth of planning had led up to this day, and we were all nervous with anticipation, especially me. It was the day I had been looking forward to and dreading at the same time. It was the day I was giving away my one and only daughter, my baby girl. My heart was filled with so much emotion. My little girl was all grown up now. Where had the years gone? Even now, why did I still see her as this adorable two-year-old?

The more I thought about it, the more I realized that my daughter had always been my pride and joy. She was special for a lot of reasons. For one thing, she was the *first* girl born into the Myers family in forty years. Talk about big news! I can still hear my two sisters cheering enthusiastically when the big announcement was made, proclaiming that "the streak had finally been broken!"

Now it was her big day. I was praying I wouldn't fall apart and make a fool out of myself. But at this point there were no guarantees.

"Are you ready for the first look?" my wife asked me. "It's going to be the first time you'll see your baby in her wedding dress." I started to get a lump in my throat and headed toward the front of the hotel. When I got there, I was told to turn around. When my daughter arrived, I turned to face her, and I gasped. How did my wife and I produce such a beautiful young lady? She was strikingly pretty and appeared so happy. It warmed my heart. I have to admit I also fought back a few tears.

"Are you ready for all this, Dad?" she asked.

I smiled. "As ready as I'll ever be, honey."

At that point we proceeded to have dozens of pictures taken of the two of us and then made our way to the church. But not just any church. The wedding was going to be at St. John the Baptist Cathedral in downtown Savannah, the most beautiful church I have ever been in (which includes the Vatican). For many years, St. John the Baptist has been a very popular wedding site, booked by couples from around the world. The French Gothic cathedral is also rich in history, having been a fixture in the local area for over one hundred years. On this wonderful October day, the cathedral never looked better.

A few minutes after arriving at St. John the Baptist, it was time for the family members to process and be seated. I was getting increasingly nervous and pretty emotional. But I promised myself and my daughter that I would not fall apart. Easier said than done.

Then it was time.

As we proceeded down the aisle, I kept thinking about how happy she was and how pleased I was with my daughter's choice in a husband. My new son-in-law was an impressive young man who really loved my daughter. That was good enough for me. Still, it was hard. I kept thinking about how grown up my little girl was now. I also thought about the tie she gave me to wear in the wedding. It was so beautiful, and the inscription on the back said, "I loved you first." It was getting more difficult to keep it together.

Finally, it was time for me to hand off my daughter and let my baby go. It was a beautiful wedding, and when the Mass came to a close, I couldn't stop my mind from wandering. I was so happy for my daughter, but I also knew that this wasn't the only baby I would have to let go. There was the matter of my other baby, the one I had to let go in the next few days. That was my other pride and joy—my business.

I started Interactive Solutions (ISI) over twenty years ago, in 1996, and built the company literally from dirt. I've always had a lot of pride in being the all-American entrepreneur who risked everything to chase the dream. Getting the business off the ground had been full of obstacles—not the least of which was getting fired from my job on my thirty-ninth birthday and having no money to start a business in the first place. Then it was securing and losing financing, overcoming a melanoma diagnosis, and dealing with a supplier embezzlement of over fifteen thousand dollars. And that was just in the first nine months. The challenges kept coming when a year later I went through a business divorce and had to buy out my partner. It was scary to take on that much debt when the company still wasn't making any money.

But I was determined that ISI would not just survive but thrive. Over the next few years, that's exactly what happened. ISI's videoconferencing and audio-visual business dramatically grew, particularly in the distance learning and telemedicine markets. Growing a business was so much fun—not just for me but for my team as well. Those were exciting times for sure.

Despite our success, there was also that little matter in 2003 when our accounting manager embezzled $257,000 from the company a short time after my brother died. When I discovered the theft, it became the day my business almost died, too.

Just four years later, in the summer of 2007, we had yet another business near-death experience when we lost 80 percent of our sales team to turnover right before the Great Recession. Talk about timing!

And despite the overwhelming obstacles, we dusted ourselves off, rebuilt the company, and doubled sales to twenty-five million amidst the worst economy in eighty years. To this day, I still think it's an incredible success story.

ISI had so many challenges and obstacles through the years, yet we met each and every one of them head on and succeeded against all odds. I was so incredibly proud of what we had built at ISI, particularly because the path to success had not been easy. ISI was way more than just a business to me. It was highly personal and a tremendous source of pride that was hard to describe. But on my daughter's wedding day, I had to accept the fact that in four days, I would be handing off my company. It was time to let my other baby go.

Selling a business you started and worked hard to grow for a number of years is a deeply personal and emotional experience. Yet when I did my initial research on the topic, I discovered that although quite a few books were available on starting a business, securing financing, marketing, and growing a business, very few dealt specifically with selling a business.

That is why I wrote this book. I wrote it to fill a void in the market and help educate other small business owners and entrepreneurs about the merger and acquisitions (M&A) process, whether they choose to sell their business or not. It's that important. Some of the topics addressed in this book include the following:

- When is the right time to sell a business?
- What does the merger and acquisition process really look like?
- How do you prepare your company for the sale?
- What can an owner do to increase the value of their company?

- How do you continue to run a business when you're actively trying to sell it?
- What about the emotional side of selling a business? How hard is it, really?
- What lessons did I learn from starting and growing a tech company for over twenty years?

Selling your business is likely to be the biggest deal of your career. And since it is so important to get it right, there is very little tolerance for error. In *Rounding Third and Heading for Home*, you'll get a firsthand look at the many components that go into the sale of your business from someone who has actually gone through it—including what to do and what *not* to do. You'll discover why it is so important to sell a business when it's ready and not necessarily when you're ready—and how to know when it's ready. You'll get an in-depth look at what really builds value in your business and understand that it's based not on what you think your business is worth but on what somebody is willing to pay for it. You'll also learn how important it is to sell the future of your business, not the past, if you want to get the maximum value.

In short, you'll find lots of real-life stories and insights to help you "touch all the bases" and achieve the success you've always dreamed of. I've always been told that entrepreneurship isn't about the destination but the journey. I hope you enjoy reading about my journey, and that it empowers yours.

*Walking my daughter Katie down the aisle
on that wonderful October afternoon.*

Chapter 1

Don't Take Your Eye Off the Ball

Obstacles are those frightful things you see when you take your eyes off of your goals.

—Henry Ford

I remember our sales meeting in December 1999 like it was yesterday. We were all gathered in the conference room of our new office in Collierville, which at one time was a beauty shop. Swanky? Not exactly. Our office was not only very spartan, it also had an annoying habit of leaking every time it rained. And I do mean every time. I remember it being so bad that every time it rained our systems engineer would put his computer on the very top of his cubicle to keep it from getting wet. Pretty crazy, but that office was all ISI could afford at the time, and we all knew we had to keep bootstrapping until the company turned the corner—whenever that might be.

We were all wondering what the next year was going to look like. There was no doubt about it: we were still struggling, and our future looked uncertain. *What are we going to do about it?* I thought. *Doesn't every business need to set goals to move forward, to have something to shoot for?*

That's when I stood up and made a statement to my team: "If we could sell two million next year, the company might just make some money."

I paused. "What do you guys think? Can we do it?"

They looked at me as if I were out of my mind.

For me, it didn't seem like a lofty goal, but the reality was that company sales had been hovering around one million or so for several years in a row and we simply weren't moving the needle. We had been doing business for over three years now, so ISI could no longer consider itself a startup. As much as we hated to admit it, we were still failing to turn a profit. Truth be told, I was getting more than a little frustrated about it.

Then the mind games started: *Was starting this company a bad idea? Are we ahead of our time selling videoconferencing in such a conservative market? Is it really worth the risk? What if ISI fails? What impact will that have on me and my family?*

A lot of hard questions with no easy answers. Times like these reminded me that doubt can be a nasty enemy. Also, beyond the doubt, I could no longer deny that both the company and I were at a crossroads. Something had to happen. So, the questions in my mind continued: *Was ISI really going to make it? When would we finally get some traction and turn the corner?*

Then I started thinking back: Wasn't it just a few years ago that we struggled to get the financing to start the business, bought out our investment partners, and survived not only my melanoma diagnosis but also a fifteen-thousand-dollar supplier embezzlement? Then there was that matter of buying out my partner and going hopelessly into debt when ISI still wasn't making money. I remember "eating stress for breakfast" in those days. *When was all this bad stuff going to end? Was it ever going to get any better?*

Now we were approaching the year 2000, which was the year of the infamous Y2K scare when so many people feared that their computers would not interpret the "00" date correctly and would stop working on December 31, 1999. In fact, many companies in the Memphis area did a great deal of planning and spent a lot of money in their IT departments to prepare for the so-called "Millennium Bug." And the crazy part of the Y2K crisis was the frightening amount of expense it took for so many companies to fix it. Assessments of the cost to Memphis companies ranged from hundreds of thousands of dollars for smaller- to medium-sized businesses to many millions of dollars for the Fortune 500 companies. Suffice it to say the Y2K crisis made selling videoconferencing equipment in the IT space even that much more difficult for ISI. We learned the hard way that it was tough growing a company with so much chaos and uncertainty swirling around.

Riding the Wave

But once the year began and the Y2K crisis was averted, a strange phenomenon occurred. After the first of the year, as we were trying to pull ISI's 2000 sales plan together, the customer and prospect calls rolled in. It was totally unexpected. It began with a few calls, and then the calls came in more frequently, one after another. For whatever reason, all of a sudden, every customer or prospect we had ever called on in the past three years seemed to be contacting us at the same time. The conversations were very similar: "Mr. Myers, remember that proposal you sent me a few years ago? Can you or someone on your team update it for me? We're ready to move on it." Others simply asked, "How long will it take to get delivery on our videoconferencing equipment?"

Is this really happening? I asked myself. I had no clue what was going on, but I sure wasn't going to look a gift horse in the mouth. Even with all the sales activity and customer requests, I constantly preached to my team, "Let's just put our heads down and focus on the work." No questions asked.

Let's ride the wave as long as we can, I thought. Since we simply weren't used to it, the hardest part of 2000 was keeping up with the crazy increase in demand. It made for some really long hours, working way past five o'clock and on the weekends as well. *Is this when all our hard work and perseverance is finally going to pay off? Is this what success looks like?* If it was, it sure had a nice feel to it, and all of us wanted to keep it going.

As the calls continued to come in, ISI got another serious boost of momentum later that year from two of our major accounts—in the same month. After many years of hard work and persistence, both FedEx and Oak Ridge National Labs (ORNL) informed us that ISI had been awarded various videoconferencing/audio-visual contracts that totaled well over two million dollars. Little old ISI was going to outfit the brand-new FedEx worldwide headquarters in Memphis with the latest in videoconferencing technology. On top of that, we would be doing much of the same for numerous ORNL laboratory locations all across the country, which included places like Los Alamos, San Francisco, New York, and Chicago. I almost couldn't believe it. I felt like I was having an out-of-body experience.

Then it hit me. "We are on to something, guys," I proclaimed at one sales meeting. "Screw this survival stuff; let's thrive! Let's raise the bar and grow this thing, gang!"

And that is exactly what we did. In fact, we didn't just settle for selling two million that year. We blew past that number and booked over $4.3 million in revenue in 2000. At the end of the year, I remember remarking to my wife, "Honey, I think we may have finally turned the corner. I think we actually have a real business now."

"Thank God," she replied. Then she said, "I always knew you could do it." That statement meant the world to me then—and now.

Starting to Get Noticed

Even though I didn't want to jinx things, after four long years the gamble really *was* looking like it was starting to pay off. So many major corporations, hospitals, and universities bought our videoconferencing, distance learning, and telemedicine systems that year it was mind boggling. And candidly, that was half the fun of it. We were all doing so many things we had never done before and enjoying every minute. As we reflected on all that was happening, my whole team and I agreed that after so many long years, ISI had finally established a solid brand in the Southeast US market and was poised for growth. With that growth, many people and organizations took notice.

For instance, one organization, the *Memphis Business Journal,* recognized ISI as the "Small Business of the Year" in March 2001. We were so excited to receive that award. And that recognition from the local business community reinforced our belief that even though it was fun to sell stuff all across the country, it was still important to take care of our backyard. Later that year, ISI earned its most prestigious recognition after we grew the business 1,541 percent over the previous five years and placed #182 on the *Inc.* 500 list of the fastest growing private companies in the United States.

Pretty cool to be on a list that at one time included companies like Microsoft, Oracle, Under Armour, and Timberland. Naturally, making the *Inc.* 500 list greatly increased ISI's visibility both regionally and nationwide. We couldn't have paid for better publicity. Now people around the country were taking notice of ISI's success.

It was on the heels of this recognition that I started getting the calls. It seemed like every investment banker and private equity firm in the United States was trying to talk to me about ISI and our plans for the future. It was also pretty clear to me that most of them had gotten ISI's name off of the *Inc.* list, which made us a likely target. All of them basically had the same pitch: "Mr. Myers, we would like to talk to you about ISI's growth strategy because we'd like to make an investment in your company." Others said, "We are really impressed with what ISI is doing with videoconferencing technology and think there is some big-time growth potential." Still others would ask, "Would you ever consider a potential acquisition of ISI and taking some chips off the table for you and your wife?" I wasn't 100 percent sure what that really meant, but it did give me something to consider. Was this the right time to cash out? Or should we press on and take the company as far as we could—in other words, should we "be all we could be"?

It seemed the calls would never end. Although it was very flattering to have people across the country interested in the company, it was also very distracting. I had the same conversation with so many of these folks over and over again: "Yes, we had a great year in 2000 and are working hard to continue growing the company," I would remark, and "No, I don't have any interest in selling the company at this time, but I appreciate your interest in ISI."

It would have been so easy to take my eye off the ball and let my mind wander. With so many people talking about ISI, it was hard not to. Given the circumstances, who wouldn't have illusions of grandeur, of getting the big check and staging a glorious exit?

After some soul searching, I knew in my heart I had to discipline myself not to get caught up in the hype and to keep working on growing the company. What did my father always say? "Don't believe all of your press clippings." Easier said than done. For so many entrepreneurs (like me), thriving on recognition is in our DNA. We love getting our egos stroked. In many cases, it's what we live for.

Plus, when you have someone interested in buying a company you built out of dirt, you're not only flattered but also curious. *If I ever did want to sell, how much could I get?* At the end of the day, every entrepreneur wants validation that the company they have worked so hard to build has some kind of value. That is one of several reasons why the many opportunities from high-powered investment firms across the country were so tempting.

Yet I had to remind myself that ISI was getting all this attention mostly because of one good year. "Can we do it again?" I asked myself and my team. "Is our success sustainable? Are we a one-hit wonder?" Those kinds of questions, coupled with an overwhelming feeling of uncertainty, helped me realize that not only was ISI *not* ready to be acquired, I wasn't personally ready either.

Timing Is Everything

Even more important than the question of value was the question of timing. I'm not going to lie. It was fun getting all those calls and engaging with potential investors. However, even if you can fool some people some of the time, you can't fool yourself. I could see ISI still had a lot of opportunity to grow, and I felt our best days were ahead of us. We were on to something and needed to see it through. I had to recognize that I was way too busy trying to *grow* my business to focus on trying to *sell* it. I needed to keep my eye on the ball.

Even though the timing wasn't right, it got me thinking about the process of acquisition and how little I knew about it. It seemed to me that selling your business was the biggest deal of your life, and it shouldn't be taken lightly. If I ever seriously considered selling ISI, how would it impact ISI employees, customers, and suppliers? These were serious questions I simply didn't have answers to. Hell, I didn't even know the right questions.

So, after a lot of careful thought, I took a deep breath and decided to get educated. How else would I know if an acquisition would ever be right for ISI? At the end of 2001, when the investor calls finally started slowing down, I began attending the various M&A seminars in the area, primarily to learn more about the M&A world and how it might impact ISI's future. Here are just a few things I learned at this early stage.

I became familiar with key terms such as *EBITDA* (earnings before interest, taxes, depreciation, and amortization), the primary benchmark in the M&A world. Essentially, EBITDA is a way to evaluate a company's operating performance without having to factor in financing decisions, accounting decisions, or tax environments.

I also became familiar with another term in the M&A process known as the LOI, or *letter of intent*. In some cases it is also called a letter of understanding or memorandum of understanding. It's not really an offer but more the starting point of a discussion that eventually lists the basic terms of a possible agreement. I also found out that it is an important first step for both parties to gauge each other's interest in putting a deal together.

Additionally, I learned why entrepreneurs need to look at *recasting* their financials in order to portray the company's true net income. So many entrepreneurs and small business owners tend to run personal expenses through the company (cars, vacations, country club memberships, etc.), which distorts the company's net income. It is also commonplace for the potential acquirer to make recast adjustments, also sometimes referred to as add-backs, pro forma adjustments, or normalization adjustments. In addition to personal expenses (noted above), the owner's compensation is also part of the recast process, which in the end creates an income statement that represents the true value of the company to the potential acquirer.

And there was still so much more to this game. I learned about the importance of the *due diligence process* and how involved it can be. Due diligence is almost like a fact-finding mission for a potential acquirer to confirm all facts about the company; this includes a review of their financials which need to be audited (not compiled) in order to more accurately represent the financial strength of the company to the acquirer. Also, I discovered that when a deal gets to the due diligence stage it can be time consuming for small business owners to secure so much information. But it is also a key step in the M&A process and needs to be fully completed before either party enters into a more formal agreement.

Some of the items on a due diligence checklist include compliance issues, information technology equipment inventory lists, company publicity, outsourced professionals (lawyers, accountants, etc.) business and health insurance coverage, any outstanding litigation, a complete listing of the company's product and services, company customer lists and company purchasing history, tax information (outstanding issues), company licenses and permits, as well as details on intellectual property (software, patents, etc.), employees/benefits (401Ks, etc.), company financial information (audited), and the run rate of revenue streams. As you can see, the process can be arduous, requiring you to retrieve so much information while you're still trying to run your business.

Other M&A terms I learned about include *net working capital calculations*, and *pegs* or *true ups* (the net working capital target)—all typically left until later stages of an M&A deal but important parts of the acquisition process. For example, I was told that millions of dollars are at stake in the true-up process, yet, for the most part, most small business owners don't really understand it. In addition to these terms, I also got a better understanding of what companies look for in a potential acquisition target, as well as the difference between a strategic and financial buyer. I also learned that some acquisitions are based on geographic location.

It was like drinking from a fire hose and learning a whole new language. At the same time, a lot of it made sense to me. And the more seminars I attended, the more I realized how much went into the M&A process—and that ISI still had a long way to go.

At least for myself, I wanted to continue to build the value of ISI so that if and when the time was right, the number wouldn't just make sense for the investor; it would make sense for me, my family, and my employees. So, I set out to build the value of our company, and in many ways, I ended up building value by simply doing what came naturally. In fact, now that I look back on it, the value of ISI was being built way back when I was a child, in the way I was raised.

Swing for the Fences

- Although it is flattering to get calls from investors and potential acquirers, stay focused on the business at hand. Don't get caught up in all the M&A talk, which can be distracting. Keep your eye on the ball.

- Get educated about the M&A process whether you have a desire to sell your company in the future or not. Attending M&A seminars can provide a keener understanding of what a potential buyer is looking for in an acquisition and better prepare you to talk with potential acquirers.

- Keep in mind that most M&A activity and acquisitions are all about timing. Remember to sell your business when *it's* ready, not when *you're* ready.

- Your business's value is based not on what you think it is worth but on what somebody is willing to pay for it.

Chapter 2
Not Born on Third Base

I'm sure you know a lot of people who were born into privilege and amounted to absolutely nothing. We all have greatness within us. So it is really important for everyone to figure out what God put us on Earth to do.

—Farrah Gray

I was the fifth of seven children, born at Our Lady of the Lake hospital in Baton Rouge, Louisiana, on December 8, 1956. That day also happened to be my father's fortieth birthday. I remember my grandmother telling me repeatedly that my father and I weren't just born on the same day but the same day of the week and just hours apart. My father and I were always close. I was also told repeatedly that of all the Myers children I was the one most like my father.

As for the rest of the family, I had two older brothers, two older sisters, and two younger brothers. My oldest sister and I were nine years apart, and my youngest brother and I were four years apart. Even though the numbers didn't add up exactly right, I was always considered the middle child. I used to tell my younger brothers that it took my parents all those years dealing with my older siblings to finally get it right. We were all part of the Baby Boomer generation born after World War II and the classic big, Catholic family. Growing up in Baton Rouge, it didn't take me long to notice that a whole lot of families in our neighborhood looked a lot like ours.

The Magnolia Woods subdivision in East Baton Rouge Parish was your typical middle-class neighborhood in those days, with lots of young, growing families trying to raise their kids and make ends meet. It was a constant struggle for many, and my family was in the same boat with everybody else. We thought having seven kids in the family was a big deal, until we discovered more than a few families with nine, ten, or even eleven kids. Now, those were big families.

Growing up, there was always a lot of love but very little money. That's just the way it was, and we knew nothing else. I remember my father remarking several times that early in his career he had an opportunity to make a lot of money in the advertising industry, but it would have required a lot of overnight travel and being away from home for extended periods of time. Even though we could have used the money, my father simply didn't want to be away from his family that long. So, his career took another direction, and he went on to have a Hall of Fame forty-plus-year career with the Better Business Bureau. Years later, he used to tell people, "In my career, I decided to make kids, not money." And that's exactly what he and my mother did.

Learning the Value of a Dollar

With seven kids and two adults, even the simplest of things was a challenge, like eating dinner together. With so many kids crowded around the dinner table, every time food was being passed around, you had to make your move very quickly or you'd get a fork in your hand. That's likely when I first developed my competitive streak. In my house, it was every man for himself, so we all had to learn how to take care of ourselves. Don't get me wrong; big families are such a blessing and can bring a whole lot of joy. But looking back on it, my family was so big that truthfully some of us didn't get to know each other very well.

It's not like my siblings and I grew up in poverty. Not at all. My father was in public service and the main breadwinner as the president of the Better Business Bureau. He made a decent salary and was well respected in the community. In addition to raising seven kids, my mother also pitched in by selling *Highlights for Children* magazine part time. Both my mother and father had a strong work ethic, which was not lost on me and my siblings. Each and every day they threw their heart and soul into their work. Although money was always tight, we never lacked for anything. Not only did my siblings and I learn what hard work looked like but we also got a daily lesson in the value of a dollar and what it took to earn one.

So, no, I didn't come from family money and most definitely was not like some people who are born on third base yet think they hit a triple. Neither me nor my siblings ever had anything given to us, and we learned how to get things done the old-fashioned way. We put our head down and worked hard. And that was a blessing. I am proud to say that everything we had as a family, we had to earn. No freebies or handouts. Pure and simple. From day one, my siblings and I had to scratch and claw and pitch in wherever we could. Many times that meant not having the fanciest clothes or the latest toy for Christmas. With such a big family, we all understood we had to sacrifice at some level. But the life lessons we learned growing up went way beyond money and would prove to be invaluable when dealing with life's future challenges.

Even though my mother and father had to watch their money very carefully, they always saved enough for us to go on occasional family vacations. Of course, one of the biggest challenges we had in those days was how we would get there. Plane travel was for rich families and certainly not something the Myers family could afford. With seven kids, there was only one economical way to get to our vacation destination, and that was by car. It wasn't easy, but we somehow crammed everybody in the family station wagon and embarked on our fabulous journey. It wasn't the most elegant way to travel, but we always got there safely and had a good time.

In preparation for those vacations, my father taught me my first important business lesson: how to set up a budget. He always wanted to know exactly how much money would be required for an upcoming trip to eliminate any guesswork or confusion. Since this was way before the days of Excel spreadsheets and computers, I can still see my father calculating the cost of our trips on the back of a napkin, itemizing every expense from motel to gas to food, which he called "eats." Both my father and mother made it abundantly clear that there was one expense they simply would not pay for: souvenirs. Those were on us. Although that position seemed harsh to me at the time, their message of sound money management came through loud and clear. It also taught each of us not to rely on our parents' income but to get some kind of job so we could cover our own expenses.

Developing a Work Ethic

When we moved to Memphis in the mid-1960s, I got my first real job, which was delivering newspapers for the *East Memphis Shoppers News*. This wasn't just delivering a few newspapers—not at all. My route included delivering the *Shoppers News* to the 343 houses located throughout our neighborhood and the adjoining one. It's been almost fifty years, but I still remember what a daunting task it was to deliver so many newspapers. Even though I only had to deliver the newspapers once a week, it was back-breaking work. Week after week, after I finished my deliveries, I had to nurse my neck and feet because they were so sore, and then I'd soak myself in a warm tub to ease the pain. Even though the *Shoppers News* job didn't pay much money, I learned many things with that first job.

At that early age, I learned about the traits an employer looks for in a prospective employee. Simple things like, can I count on this employee to show up for work on time? Will they put in the effort to make sure the job is done right? Can I trust them? Are they conscientious? How do they deal with customers? I remember that issue became a big deal to me when I occasionally received complaints from customers/homeowners who got upset about "papers that were blowing."

So now I don't just have to deliver 343 newspapers; I also have to control the weather? The more I thought about it, the madder I got. *Don't these people know that this is a* free *newspaper and that I delivered it to their door?* Even the newspaper they paid for was delivered to the driveway. It didn't seem fair, but I learned a valuable business lesson: the customer is always right. That lesson served me well later in my career when I was trying to grow my own company.

After my job with the *Shoppers News,* I got another part-time job that had the potential to make me some really good money doing something entirely different. That job was walking around and selling sodas to fans at University of Memphis football games at the Liberty Bowl Memorial Stadium. I worked the entire season pretty much every Saturday afternoon or evening during my freshman year of high school in 1970. This job might not have been very glamorous, but it did teach me some valuable lessons about hustling and spotting business opportunities.

For starters, I learned that if you want to make more money, you have to learn how to work the system and be smart about it. When I first began selling sodas at the Liberty Bowl, I wasted a whole lot of time running back and forth getting a new tray every time I ran out of drinks. On top of that, I then had to wait in line with everyone else to get my tray refilled. I learned quickly that time was truly money and that working from one tray at a time was *not* the way to go. I quickly changed my strategy and stacked multiple trays at a time (as many as three) versus just taking one. While the other guys were running back up the stairs to the concession stand, I was able to stay out there and keep selling (even if my arms were hurting pretty badly from carrying three trays at a time).

I also discovered the secret to making really good money on game nights: find as many partying customers as you could. In those days, many people came to the games with their own liquor (and probably still do today). But what they usually didn't bring were mixers. When I could spot these customers in the crowd, it was a great opportunity for my soda business, and I would focus my efforts on selling to those customers, particularly the night of the Liberty Bowl game. Most of the time, these fans were enjoying themselves so much that they were tipping me five dollars for two dollars' worth of Cokes. One night I made forty dollars in one hour, which was great money for a fourteen-year-old kid. To this day, I've told people that selling Cokes at the Liberty Bowl game may have been the highest paying hour of my career if you account for inflation. Not only did I make a lot of money hustling Cokes that night, but there was also an added benefit to my success. Since I had done so well in the first half of the game, I decided to celebrate my victory in the second half by sitting down in the stands and watching the rest of the bowl game like the fans. For a teenage kid, it didn't get any better than that.

When I graduated from high school, my parents made it very clear that they did not have the money for me to attend college. My dad told me, "Your mother and I paid for you to go to one of the best high schools in the area (Christian Brothers), and we simply don't have the money to pay for you to go to college. If you want to go to college, *you* are going to have to pay for it." No rich granddad or trust fund for me.

I got the message loud and clear, so I enrolled at Memphis State University (now the University of Memphis) and immediately got part-time jobs to pay for my tuition. I had a *lot* of jobs working my way through college, ranging from grocery-store stocker to corporate mail clerk. One summer I even had a job working for Phillip Morris, test marketing some of their products. Those products mostly consisted of cigarette samples I passed out on the Mid America Mall in Memphis. Although the job actually paid pretty well, I have to admit, as a non-smoker, I was somewhat disgusted by the work I had to do. But I did what I had to do to make ends meet.

Hands down, the worst job I ever had was working for an electronics company in downtown Memphis one summer when I was a junior in college. The company had me and my co-workers hanging fiberglass insulation on the second floor of their warehouse. Every day we had to climb very tall ladders to get to where we needed to be, which wasn't too much fun for me as I have serious acrophobia. If that wasn't bad enough, the temperature in the warehouse had to be at least ninety degrees consistently. It was miserable work, but I kept telling myself that at least I was drawing a paycheck. That terrible job also served another purpose. It gave me even more motivation to get my college degree so I wouldn't have to do this kind of work again.

Maybe it took going through the worst part-time job I'd ever had to get to the best part-time job I ever had, which was when IBM hired me as a sales support assistant. My job was to support the IBM sales team by installing (and training clients) on correcting Selectric and memory typewriters all across the Mid-South. I loved my job and was so proud to have it. Here I was, a college junior going to business school, and after I left the classroom, I got to work for one of the largest technology firms in the world. On top of that, the company printed IBM business cards for me to pass out to our customers. It was a priceless opportunity to learn more about the world of sales and what it took to be successful. To be honest, it wasn't too hard to figure out. The most successful IBM sales reps all had one common trait: they all knew how to hustle and work hard. Success had no shortcuts. That experience with IBM made an indelible mark on my career as I identified what I really wanted to do in the future: work with customers and sell stuff.

Hustling to Be Successful

My first job out of college was selling offset printing equipment on straight commission, which means I was paid no salary. Instead, I was paid a draw of eight hundred dollars a month, which was essentially an advance against my future commissions. It was pretty straightforward: if I didn't sell anything that month, the draw would be charged back to me and I would go in the hole. On the other hand, when I sold something, I would earn a 18-20 percent commission on the sale and receive a check for the balance minus expenses. Selling in those days required you to essentially manage a profit and loss (P&L) statement, which was very challenging, but it did provide invaluable experience for a young guy straight out of college. It reinforced the fact that if I wanted to be successful, I would always have to outwork everybody else—and hustle.

After that, I worked in sales for large companies like Eastman Kodak and Hewlett Packard and learned even more about how to achieve success. While I was with Kodak, I learned a lot about competitive selling as well as the importance of having good presentation skills. I also learned that even a multibillion-dollar company like Kodak doesn't always have it all figured out. They particularly didn't have it figured out in the world of technology when they started and then closed the company's electronic publishing division (which I worked in) in less than a year.

Kodak's misstep really hurt the company, but it hurt me personally even more since I had just taken the job with the new division and had to relocate to North Carolina with my wife and a five-week-old baby. That's when I first got the idea of becoming an entrepreneur and owning my own business. I remember those days like they were yesterday; I thought, *I will never let a company jerk me and my family around ever again. I am going to continue to build my career and control my own destiny.*

I also realized that even though Kodak fumbled the ball, the future of business was going to be in technology. I decided I needed some solid tech experience on my resume, and that's when I took a job in sales with Hewlett Packard. HP was a company founded by two engineers (Bill Hewlett and Dave Packard) and was widely considered a market leader in the industry. But at its core, it was an engineering company, and I felt totally out of place there in sales. So, I made another career move to a regional telecom company called ATS Telephone and Data Systems, which hired me to be their data products manager. It was touted as the opportunity of a lifetime, and looking back on it almost thirty years later, that's exactly what it was. At ATS, I got introduced to videoconferencing, which subsequently changed my career and my life. My experience with ATS also laid the foundation for me to finally get control of my life and chase my dream of owning my own business.

All these years later, I have to say I would never have had the confidence to start and grow my own business had it not been for my upbringing and the lessons I learned from the way I was raised. Since I wasn't born on third base and had no family member's money to fall back on, I learned how to make it on my own. Even as a career C student, I knew that with hard work, tenacity, and persistence I could achieve anything I set my mind to. That mentality allowed me to overcome the numerous challenges and obstacles I faced in starting and growing ISI. That's the first step to building value in your business: it has to remain in existence in the first place.

Swing for the Fences

- No matter how successful you become in your life or career, never forget where you came from.
- Having a strong work ethic is the key to building a successful career and a business trait you want to be known for.
- View each job in your career as a stepping-stone that can allow you to learn, grow, and position yourself for future opportunities.
- Take chances in your career and realize that you don't achieve your dreams by always taking the safest route.

With nine of us in the family, there was never a lot of room in our house in Louisiana, but there was always a lot of love.

Chapter 3
We All Need a Mentor

A mentor is someone who allows you to see the hope inside yourself.
—Oprah Winfrey

It was just another day in the Kodak office when I got the phone call.

"Are you my new sales rep?" he asked.

"Yes, sir," I answered.

"Well, get your butt over here because I've got a bone to pick with your company! And make it quick!" he growled.

"I will be there as soon as I can," I responded nervously and quickly hung up.

That was my introduction to Jim Murphy, manager of copier services at Federal Express (now FedEx). It was the early 1980s, and I was working in sales for Eastman Kodak selling copier/duplicators in the Memphis area. Federal Express had been recently assigned to me because their former Kodak sales rep had decided to relocate to

Atlanta. Initially, I had looked forward to being assigned to the Federal Express account, with its potential to significantly enhance my sales career (and pocketbook). Now I was thinking, *What the hell have I gotten myself into?* As I made my way to Jim's office, I was more than a little concerned.

I was hoping Jim's in-person demeanor would be different than the one demonstrated on the phone call. Well, it wasn't. When I met him in his office, he was just as gruff and no-nonsense as he had been on the phone. But I also sensed something about this guy that I liked. Despite all of his bravado, I got the feeling that he was a straight shooter who would let you know where you stood at all times, a no-BS guy who didn't play games with people. He was all business, and I could deal with that.

On a fun note, I soon discovered that Jim was also a big sports fan and that he and I shared a love for both our hometown Memphis Tigers and Notre Dame. Despite our rocky start, it seemed like a marriage made in heaven.

Meeting Jim couldn't have come at a better time for me. My career at Kodak had gotten off to a rough start my first year, with very few sales and lots of pressure from management. On top of that, I had just gotten married and bought a house. Those difficult times were destroying my confidence and had me second guessing myself. I was lost. It was not a good place to be and definitely not the right mentality for a successful sales career.

Jim was like the hero from central casting who arrived just in time to save the day. He became not only my best customer but my mentor as well. When I needed it the most, Jim provided me the support and encouragement I was so desperately seeking. Looking back on it, I have to say that he believed in me before I believed in me. I learned so much about business and life from him.

Before Jim joined FedEx, he had been a sales manager at Xerox (Kodak's biggest competitor), and he constantly shared sales insights and strategies with me. Jim made me proud to be a salesman and helped me in so many ways to become a professional. He was also a lot of fun and had a wicked sense of humor. I fondly remember the advice he shared with the Kodak sales team one day when we invited him over to impart his wisdom. Jim began the meeting with his sales rule number one, which was, "Don't call your best customer a son of a b***h." We all got a chuckle out of that. He wasn't kidding. To this day, I am pretty sure he was pointing that particular piece of advice at me more than anyone else.

Jim was also very smart; having majored in math in college, he was a genius at calculating complex pricing models in his head. That led to probably the most valuable tip Jim ever gave me, which helped me not only in my sales position at the time but also in my future career: "Always know your numbers." In the copier industry, that meant having a handle on pricing options, competitive positioning, commissions totals, and more. Jim would always tell me to double and triple check my numbers, particularly when it came to business contracts and my sales commissions. "Don't assume anything when it comes to your money," he would say. "Trust but verify." Common sense, right? Well, I first learned it from Jim Murphy over thirty years ago, long before it was common sense to me. That advice proved to be invaluable years later when I became an entrepreneur.

Jim passed away a few years ago at age eighty-five, which still greatly saddens me. But his place in my life and career as my mentor will never be forgotten. My wife Maureen and I still refer to our Collierville home as "the house that Jim built." Without a doubt, I would not be where I am today if I hadn't met Jim Murphy. In this life, everyone needs a mentor, and for a very long time, I had the best. I'll always be grateful for all he did for me and my family.

Learning from a Business Legend

But Jim was not my only mentor. Years later, when ISI was in startup mode and barely three months old, I received another fateful phone call.

"Mr. Myers, this is Kemmons Wilson, and I've been reading about you and your company in the *Memphis Business Journal*. I'd like to stop by and see some of your fancy new videoconferencing technology. How does tomorrow afternoon look for you?"

I was so surprised that at first I didn't know how to reply. I thought one of my goofball friends was playing a practical joke on me. This was Kemmons Wilson, who transformed the motel industry in the early 1950s by founding the Holiday Inn chain after taking his family on the "vacation that changed the face of the American road"? Kemmons Wilson, whose success with Holiday Inn put him on the front cover of *Time* and resulted in the *London Sunday Times* naming him one of the "thousand makers of the twentieth century"? *That* Kemmons Wilson was calling me and wanted to see our technology? Really?

Once I got over the shock and realized that the voice on the other end of the phone really *was* Kemmons Wilson, I quickly made arrangements for a videoconferencing demonstration the next day. "Looking forward to meeting you in person, Mr. Wilson," I said before he hung up.

When he walked into my office the next day, sporting his Holiday Inn tie, I was so blown away that I literally had my receptionist go out and get a camera so she could take pictures of the two of us together. It was a moment frozen in time forever: the fledgling entrepreneur meets the business legend. I still have that picture of me and Mr. Wilson in my office, and it continues to be my good luck charm twenty-four years later.

After we finished showing him the technology, he gave me some parting advice: "You hang in there; you're gonna make some money with this business!" As a practicing Catholic, I thought the Pope had just blessed me.

It turned out Mr. Wilson was right. And although he never bought anything, his advice and encouragement went well beyond that one-day encounter. In fact, Mr. Wilson met with me several more times over the next few months in his office where we would discuss a wide variety of business-related issues and growth strategies. He was also incredibly curious about so many things. And I have to admit, I was more than amazed to listen to a man of his age who was still so energetic and interested in a wide range of new business ideas. As you can guess, I really enjoyed talking to him, but most of the time, I would simply listen as he mentored me on the finer points of entrepreneurship and growing a successful business. He offered one piece of advice I particularly appreciated. "When you are building your company," he told me, "make sure that you're not the one doing all the work. Find people with a skill set you don't have and then let them do their job."

"You want to grow your business and be successful?" he would ask me. "It's pretty straightforward. You can't do it all yourself so don't even try." He stressed that I should work hard to put together a leadership team I trusted, who could help me build a business for the future. It was simple advice, but it made a lot of sense to me—both then and now.

Mr. Wilson shared many tips and sayings that were part of his formula for success. First of all, we had to put in the time. "Work a half day. It makes no difference which half—it can be the first twelve hours or the last twelve hours." He also encouraged me to "never be afraid of taking a chance" and also to "remember that we all climb the ladder of success one step at a time." Finally, he said repeatedly, "Don't be a clock watcher." I'll never forget the day he told me to "sell my wristwatch and buy an alarm clock" so I could know when to start my day and not have to look back.

Kemmons Wilson was a master of motivation, and I will always appreciate the time he spent mentoring me when my company was just getting started. I truly believe that my experiences with Mr. Wilson in those early days greatly influenced ISI's future success.

Understanding the Value of Company Culture

As ISI grew, I continued to reach out to successful entrepreneurs who had been there and done that. One man I am proud to know and have continued to reach out to is Mike Bruns, who owned a company called Comtrak Logistics in Memphis. Comtrak was/is a national transportation company that offers full truckload, intermodal, depot, and logistics services and operates numerous full-service terminals throughout the country. Mike is originally from Chicago and moved to Memphis in the early 1980s. He started Comtrak in 1983 and recently retired after he sold the company in 2010.

When I first met Mike, I could tell he was a no-nonsense guy, much like Jim Murphy, and I have really enjoyed getting to know him. To this day, Mike is the kind of guy who is willing to lend an ear and provide timely advice whenever I need it. In short, Mike Bruns typifies what it means to be a mentor, and I am so thankful for all of his help and guidance through the years. As I look back, I see that Mike has played an important role in my journey as an entrepreneur.

Since my earliest days as a business owner, I've focused on building a strong leadership team and creating a solid company culture—a priority I set thanks to Kemmons Wilson and Mike Bruns. Mike always told me that even though he was the owner, he "didn't sit on a d*mn throne"; he believed it was important to treat all employees with dignity and respect. In fact, he made it a point to have coffee with all of his drivers every morning before they went on their way. That sent a message loud and clear to all of his employees: "I care about you."

"It's not that complicated, Jay," he would tell me. "Treat your employees the way you want to be treated, and they will take care of you." Just as Mr. Wilson advised me years earlier, Mike also stressed the importance of building a solid leadership team that had the skill set to grow your business.

Mike emphasized how important it was to nurture a culture that encourages creativity and where everyone in the company has a voice. As he told me many times, "When you hire good people, make sure you take the time to listen to them. You never know when one of your employees will come up with an idea or product that could take your business to the next level." That was solid advice that I took to heart, and I do believe that listening to my employees, particularly about new products and services, had a lot to do with ISI's ability to significantly grow throughout its lifespan.

So how much have I valued Mike Bruns's insights and advice through the years? Mike was one of the first people I counseled with regarding the sale of my business. He had been there, and I was certain he could provide me with valuable insight about what I was getting myself into, including the good, the bad, and the ugly aspects of an acquisition and the emotional toll it would have on me. To this day, I truly believe Mike's assistance enabled me to navigate the tricky M&A process successfully to close on the biggest deal of my career.

Becoming the Mentor

I have truly benefited both personally and professionally from the relationships I have formed with my mentors through the years. In realizing their importance to my career, I have made a concerted effort over the past few years to transition from being a mentee to being a mentor as well. To me, it didn't seem right to always be the person doing all of the taking without making the effort to give back. That is one of many reasons I have been active in the local Memphis entrepreneurial community supporting entrepreneurial organizations such as Start Co. Part venture development group, part accelerator, Start Co.'s summer of acceleration program is consistently attracting entrepreneurs from all over the country. For the past few years, I have been honored to be the keynote speaker for the Start Co. founders dinners where I have shared my personal experiences as an entrepreneur and the ups and downs of owning a business. In addition to that, I have also mentored a number of Start Co. entrepreneurs by offering professional business advice on a wide variety of problems and issues they are dealing with.

One Start Co. company I have recently worked with is Diatech Diabetes Technologies, a company that started on the campus of Florida State University. Diatech creates innovative technology for diabetes patients worldwide, and its first product is a new infusion set for insulin pumps that provides real-time alerts for insulin delivery failure at injection sites. Another is Oracle Health, a healthcare technology company based in Tampa, Florida, which is developing a miniature implantable smart stethoscope to continuously monitor heart sounds in patients at high risk for heart failure to prevent adverse events and hospitalization.

After spending time with these companies this past summer, I soon realized that both have huge potential, and I am hoping that some of my advice will have a positive impact on their future.

Besides Start Co., I have also been involved at the University of Memphis as a mentor for a number of student entrepreneurs who have started a wide array of companies, including an artisan coffee shop, a logistics company, and several companies launching trendy new clothing lines. One U of M student whom I have spent a lot of time with is Venki Mandapati who has started a company called Careerquo, an online social video platform that provides young people with virtual career advising and mentorship. Yet another company I have been working with in Memphis sells a software-based product called Positive Physics, which breaks traditional physics problems down into well-defined skill sets, thus allowing students to master all necessary skills before putting them together to solve a problem. Positive Physics focuses on conceptual reasoning and real-world examples over algebraic manipulation and abstractions. With this method, the company has experienced tremendous success in making physics accessible to all learners, especially the populations they serve in inner-city Memphis. And I do believe Positive Physics has the potential to be sold successfully across the country.

Another company I've been working with, which I also believe has huge potential, is Party Boxx. A University of Memphis business school student started this business with a mission to conceptualize and build the best Bluetooth speakers on the market. As the company motto states, "We want our customers to love our speakers as much as we do." All Party Boxx speakers are built from unique, top-quality components (like ammo cans) to ensure that the speakers will stand the test of time. Party Boxx has been selling their speakers online for the past few years and is poised for growth. The best part? The company envisions growing the business to the point that they can eventually hire military veterans to help build their speakers. I love the product, the vision, and the company slogan: "Never Leave Your Music Behind." It's exciting just to think about the possibilities for these companies. Even though I have sold my company, I've been able to stay fully immersed in the excitement of entrepreneurship through mentoring.

In my current role as executive in residence at the University of Memphis Fogelman College of Business and Economics (FCBE), I continue to be contacted by students who are interested in starting their own business, and I must say, I love it. Not only am I having a ball working with them on their businesses, but I also admire them so much for having the guts to start a business while they are still going to school. Really amazing! And as a U of M FCBE alum (class of 1978), I can 100 percent attest to the fact that I never had the nerve or the guts to start a business in my twenties as a student. The very notion of owning my own business was way too scary. That is one of the many reasons I have been so active with the Collegiate Entrepreneurs Organization (CEO) over the past ten years.

CEO was organized in part because entrepreneurship as a field of study at colleges and universities across the United States and around the world has become a leading subject at the undergraduate and graduate level. According to the 2011 Global Entrepreneurship Monitor (GEM) US Report, younger adults (ages eighteen to twenty-four) are more likely to start a business, and college graduates or those pursuing higher education are particularly more inclined to pursue entrepreneurship. With this increased attention, CEO recognizes it is more important than ever to give students opportunities to network, not only with their student peers but also with fellow entrepreneurs in the business world to promote entrepreneurship at all levels and in all environments.

The organization was founded in Chicago in 1983 and is now headquartered in Tampa. CEO currently supports more than 16,500 emerging collegiate entrepreneurs annually, and it believes that any student, regardless of academic discipline, can launch a business. I have been heavily involved with CEO, particularly in the past decade. In that time I have mentored dozens of start-up entrepreneurs who attend universities from all across the country, which has been so gratifying. I am also proud to say that a few years ago I even helped get the CEO chapter started at my alma mater (the University of Memphis).

For me, being a mentor to these young people is truly a labor of love, which I hope to continue for many years to come. In my mind, it's the least I can do to help the next generation of entrepreneurs. Because, in the end, we all need a mentor. Looking back, I have to say that mentoring has truly been one of the high points of my career. Also, I do believe that by paying it forward and helping others succeed, you can leave an indelible mark on people's lives and your community for many years to come.

Swing for the Fences

- Successful people almost always have a mentor who helped them along the way.
- Mentors have experience and knowledge you can learn from, so seek them out. There is great value in listening to someone who has been there, done that.
- Mentors are a valuable resource who can offer timely encouragement to keep you going. They can also be a great source of objective advice in dealing with business problems.
- Pay it forward by becoming a mentor to young entrepreneurs and help them chase their dreams. It is likely the most rewarding thing you'll ever do in your career.

My wife Maureen and I with my mentor Jim Murphy. Although he could be difficult at times, Jim had a heart of gold and taught me so much about business and life.

*I really enjoy mentoring young entrepreneurs like Venki Mandapati.
Such an impressive young man with a bright future!*

Chapter 4

Knowing Your Brand

A brand for a company is like a reputation for a person. You earn reputation by trying to do hard things well.
—Jeff Bezos

B ack in 1996, when I started ISI, a number of companies were selling videoconferencing technology, most of them large worldwide organizations with a ton of resources. Here I was, a teeny-tiny company with a whopping three employees, trying to compete with them. We had to develop a strategy merely to compete and survive.

Since we didn't have the resources and buying power of the larger firms, what advantage did we have? Who were we? How did we want to be perceived in the technology marketplace?

Focus on What You Have

Rather than focus on what we didn't have, we decided to focus on what we did have. And what we did have was a wealth of experience (over fifteen years) in an industry that was still very much in its infancy. Our goal was not just to provide hardware and software. We sought to position ourselves as subject matter experts who could not only handle questions about videoconferencing systems *but also* provide technical assistance with complicated data networking and connectivity issues.

Keep in mind that in 1996 this industry was not only still very new and mysterious, but it also had more than its share of technical challenges and obstacles. Also, at the time, our competitors were mostly large telecom companies, such as Bell South and AT&T, that were quite busy selling PBX telephone switches, voice mail systems, networks, and more. In other words, selling videoconferencing systems was not their primary business, and, therefore, they weren't very good at it. That's when we recognized an opportunity to develop our brand.

Like many bleeding-edge technologies, videoconferencing generated a lot of interest, but we soon discovered that our customers and prospects had more questions about the technology than answers. That's where ISI came in. Early on, we spent a lot of time educating the market about what the technology could and couldn't do. The more complex the application, the better for us since we were developing our brand and leveraging our expertise. We were playing our game and not the competition's game, and that made it a lot of fun. That, in turn, also created an industry opportunity for a niche player like ISI. Years later, we kidded about being like a PT boat going up against the aircraft carriers. The truth was, we won a lot of business because we played to our strengths, and thus a brand was born.

We worked hard to develop our brand one day at a time, which in the next few years morphed into selling more advanced videoconferencing applications like distance learning and telemedicine.

Those applications dramatically grew ISI's revenue for a number of years and ultimately helped us turn the corner to profitability. I have to admit, those were some really fun days at ISI. We were rapidly growing the business by knowing who we were and aggressively marketing our brand. Our motto in those days was, "We're not trying to conquer the whole world. We're trying to conquer *our* world." We did that by knowing our brand.

Stick to What You're Good At

That strategy worked for many years at ISI—until we ran into one of the biggest obstacles our company (and many other companies) had ever faced: the Great Recession. It was the worst economic downturn in a generation, lasting for almost two years (2007–2009). Like many companies, ISI was scrambling just to make payroll, keep the lights on, and remain solvent. Every day was a challenge. Amidst all the fear and uncertainty in the marketplace, it was hard to stay focused. Like many entrepreneurs, I found it hard to think about growing my business when we didn't know what the next day would look like.

That's when another obstacle crept into our psyche: doubt. Doubt can be a nasty enemy. "Should we keep selling AV and videoconferencing equipment, or should we get into some other technology?" I asked our team. "Maybe we need to get into cell phones or PCs . . . you know, something people will use every day." I got a very lukewarm response, which should have told me something. As I thought more about diversification, I was forced to realize that selling something other than videoconferencing was getting away from the ISI brand. And that was a scary thought.

But drastic times require drastic measures, so out of necessity, ISI seriously contemplated going into some other lines of business. We knew it could be risky, but we felt we had to do whatever it took to keep the company going.

As I was agonizing over all of this, I got a call from one of our best customers at FedEx.

"Jay, I have a number of AV/videoconferencing projects I would like ISI to quote on. Are you guys geared up to take care of me? I could really use your help."

"Of course we'll help you," I responded, but internally I was hesitating. It's not like I didn't appreciate the opportunity for work, but I simply wasn't as focused on AV and videoconferencing at the time. My mind kept wandering to ISI's future, mulling over what the next move for the company was going to be. Was this the time to get serious about getting into some other technologies?

He must have noticed the hesitation in my voice because he called me on it.

"What's the issue?" he asked. I confessed that I was very uncertain about what direction to take the company in to survive the recession. I told him my head was spinning, and truthfully, I was way off my game.

To this day, I will never forget his response. He said, "Jay, it's not that complicated. Just stick to what you're good at and keep doing more of it."

Just like that, one of my best customers gave me my game plan for the future. In fact, it was so simple, I thought, *Why didn't I think of that?* Plus, what could be better than getting business advice from your biggest customer? Certainly, his advice was in his own best interest at FedEx, but he also believed in ISI and wanted to see us successfully grow the company into the future. So, we took his advice to heart, stuck to what we were good at, and stayed true to our brand.

It turned out his advice was not only simple but priceless. From 2007 to 2011, we more than doubled our business from eleven million to twenty-five million amidst the worst economy in eighty years. It was all because we stuck to our guns, stayed focused, and continued to promote our brand.

Make No Apologies for Who You Are

A few years ago, ISI was engaged in an intense battle to win a two million dollar AV contract at a large international corporate account I had personally been chasing for more than twenty years. Several dozen companies from across the country were competing for the business, many of which were much larger than ISI and had resources we could only dream of. Could a firm our size go to toe-to-toe with our competition and win?

Against all odds, ISI was one of a few firms that made it to the final cut, which thrilled all of us. Upon notification from corporate purchasing, we were then asked to meet with various project managers and IT team leaders (again) to review some issues. Although we were apprehensive about the meeting, we all agreed that we had to put our best foot forward in presenting our proposal. From the moment we sat down, we noticed a lot of tension in the room; it was very evident that the corporate sourcing and procurement managers just wanted to talk about one thing: pricing. From the outset of the meeting, we were challenged on almost every line item in our proposal.

After listening patiently for several minutes, I finally asked the sourcing manager to stop, and then I posed a simple question: "Jerry, what kind of company do you think you guys are dealing with? Do y'all think ISI is like Walmart, and we're all running around with blue vests and talking about providing 'everyday low prices'?" At that point, I was on a roll, and I finally told them, "If that's what you are looking for, then we need to end the meeting and adjourn for an early lunch. However, if you are looking for a company that provides good pricing and even better service and support, then we're your guys."

I'll never forget the look on my team members' faces. They were so stunned they couldn't even speak. I asked myself, *Did I just say what I think I said? Did I blow this whole opportunity?*

After what seemed like an eternity, the sourcing manager looked at me, cleared his throat, and said, "Okay, we do need good pricing, but we also need to hear about how your company can service and support this contract." It was the answer we needed, and I was thrilled to hear it.

When my team and I left the meeting, my VP of design/engineering turned to me and said, "I don't know what you had for breakfast this morning, but keep eating it!" That comment reminded me of one of the single most important things a business owner must do: know your brand and stand behind it. If you as the owner don't know how to communicate your brand, then how do you expect your employees to do it?

It doesn't take a genius to figure out that most smaller firms cannot compete in a price war with clients and prospects. The bigger firms have always had the advantage of deeper discounts and greater resources; it's as simple as that. But I do believe small- and mid-sized firms need to focus on their strengths, not their weaknesses. In our case, although we weren't able to match our competitors' pricing line item by line item, we did offer the client local project management, exceptional customer service, and support. With a project worth over two million dollars (which included new construction), that was a big deal.

So, what happened next? After days of further evaluation, we got the call that we were the chosen vendor for the project. Great news for us. But it also reinforced the importance of knowing your brand. In our case, our brand was not (nor has it ever been) about being the low-cost provider; instead, we were a highly respected company that focused on quality of work and ongoing customer service and support. In the end, ISI won a big contract because we stuck to our guns and recognized who we were. And we had an industry brand that would serve us for many years to come.

By the way, you can communicate your brand with more than just words. After we won that two-million-dollar contract, we got some interesting feedback about the firm's decision-making process. They told us ISI was not the lowest bidder on the project, but our local support was extremely important to them. In addition to the local support advantage, they also told us they were impressed with the way we were dressed when we did our final presentation. In fact, the corporate project manager made it a point to tell me how impressed they were that the entire ISI team showed up for the meeting decked out in suits and ties (even the techies). Apparently, our team looked very different from our competitors, who had all dressed casually. According to the manager, we all looked like "we had stepped out of the boardroom and meant business," which was right in line with our brand of being a highly respected company.

Today I've noticed that many small business owners tend to focus on cash flow, personnel, and other day-to-day concerns rather than on what got them there in the first place: their brand. From a practical standpoint, based on my experience, a strong company brand is what creates value in the business, whether you're a startup or you've been in business for twenty years. An often-quoted slogan in business is "our people make the difference," and that's true for both your customers and your employees. Your customers benefit from employees who serve them consistently and well, and your employees benefit from being treated consistently and well within the company.

Also, based on my recent personal experience in the M&A world, I have found that acquirers (particularly in the tech industry) are primarily looking for a strong company brand based on technical knowledge and expertise (programming, software, etc.) rather than products and hardware. By building a strong company brand based on knowledge and intellectual property, you not only distinguish your business from your competition but also position yourself for the future, whatever opportunities it may bring.

Swing for the Fences

- Having a strong brand is what distinguishes you from your competition and is the key to building a successful business. Protect your brand at all costs.

- It's important that everyone in your company understands your brand and can articulate it on a regular basis.

- A company's brand increases the value of the company and provides direction and motivation for employees. It also makes acquiring new customers easier.

- A strong company brand encourages employee loyalty and can be both a retention and recruiting tool.

Chapter 5
The Art and Science of Professional Selling

Sales is not about selling anymore, but about building trust and educating.

—Siva Devaki

Q: What's the difference between a computer salesman and a used-car salesman?

A: The used-car salesman knows when he's lying.

N early everyone has a bad salesperson joke in their back pocket. Yet surveys show many Fortune 500 CEOs got their start in sales.[1] Pretty impressive for a profession that is often misunderstood and, in many cases, disrespected.

In fact, many entrepreneurs say their start in sales was a vital ingredient in their later business success. Mark Cuban, for example, began his career selling garbage bags. As the story goes, Mark's father told him that if he wanted a new pair of tennis shoes, he had to earn the money himself to buy them. Sounds a lot like my father. So, after doing some research, Cuban came up with the idea to do some old-fashioned selling. He would go door to door to sell garbage bags. Why garbage bags? After doing his homework, Cuban discovered that many people had a need for cheaper garbage bags and didn't want to make the trip to the store to purchase them. After a few weeks, Cuban earned the money for his tennis shoes. Talk about enterprising. It's no wonder that later on Cuban became the founder of the startup internet radio company Broadcast.com, which he sold to Yahoo! for $5.7 billion back in 1999. He is currently starring in the hit reality TV show *Shark Tank*.[2]

Interestingly enough, Howard Schultz, chairman and CEO of Starbucks, started his career in the copier/duplicator industry (just like me), working in sales at Xerox's one-hundred-million-dollar headquarters in Virginia. It was there that Schultz was introduced to the Professional Sales Skills course (PSS), which he continues to tout as the best sales training in the country—and I'll talk more about it below. By leveraging his Xerox PSS training, Schultz became a top sales producer, and it was this sales experience that helped him build the Starbucks brand into a worldwide phenomenon.[3]

When I took my first job as a salesman after graduating from college, I had no idea how well that experience would prepare me for my big leap to entrepreneurship twenty years later. I learned early on in my career that for any business to be successful, someone has to sell something. It isn't that complicated. And through the years, I also learned that many of the qualities of a successful salesperson are the same for a successful entrepreneur, including competitiveness, enthusiasm, resiliency, confidence, and the ability to network. Years later I learned I would need to leverage these qualities and several more to start and grow my own business.

As I mentioned earlier, before I started ISI, I sold for both Hewlett Packard and a regional telecom firm where I was first introduced to videoconferencing. Before that, I worked over six years for Eastman Kodak, selling high-speed copier/duplicators, and for AM International, selling printing equipment. Looking back, I have been in professional sales for over forty years and have been fortunate to achieve success with each and every company I worked for.

In fact, I would say that my sales experience was instrumental in building a successful career. Why? Here are just a few reasons.

Both Entrepreneurship and Sales Require 100 Percent Effort

I already had a strong work ethic, but sales took it to a whole new level. In the early days of my career, when I was selling copiers, my sales manager expected me to be making at least twenty face-to-face calls a week—and more if I could do it. I was also expected to cold call on as many companies as possible, which included starting at the top floor of an office building and working my way to the bottom floor, passing out business cards to anyone who would take them. And this was expected week after week and month after month.

I learned that although sales could be a really fun job, it also required a lot of good old-fashioned hard work. Sales is all about the hustle, and you have to give it maximum effort to be successful. I also learned that sales is all about the numbers, and either you produce those or you don't. It's very cut and dry. And there are no shortcuts. You have to have the discipline to call on enough customers and prospects to build a funnel that produces the desired sales results. In other words, you have to make your quota. I learned this important skill set early on. Truthfully, I feel like I have been on some kind of quota my whole life!

I had no idea how well my sales experience would prepare me for the life of an entrepreneur. I learned through the years that it didn't matter whether I was selling copiers back in the day or building my own business; success requires 100 percent effort. You simply have to do what it takes for as long as it takes to get the job done.

Entrepreneurs Are Always Selling

In the early days of building ISI, I had to utilize my professional selling skills to literally get the business off the ground. That meant I had to sell the idea of taking a chance on us to our initial private investors. I had to sell a well-respected AV engineer on joining a risky startup and becoming the technical arm of the company. It didn't stop there. In succeeding days, I had to convince various AV and videoconferencing vendors to take a chance on us as well. Maybe the most important sale I had to make in the early days was to convince the bank to approve our line of credit to operate the business. And let's not forget that I had to sell potential recruits on joining a startup business, a risky proposition at best. But you do what you have to do, and thank God I possessed the necessary sales skills to get the job done.

Sales Is a Science That Requires Training

Being a young professional in the printing/duplicator industry in the late 1970s, I was exposed to a sales training course created by our biggest competitor at the time: Xerox. The Professional Selling Skills course (PSS), also known as "Selling by Needs Satisfaction," was created inside the Xerox company in 1968. The company spent ten million dollars to develop this methodology and later created the Xerox Learning Systems division just to sell its new selling technique.

One of the fundamentals of the PSS course was being able to understand the features, advantages, and benefits of a product or service to the customer, otherwise known as the FAB process. By thoroughly understanding the FAB process, a salesperson could then go through the four phases of PSS selling, which included (1) needs identification, (2) presentation, (3) objection handling, and (4) closing.

That's when it dawned on me: there was a science behind professional sales, and I was learning techniques from the very best. Forty years later, I still say the Xerox salespeople were the best in the world. And I have to admit that I was thrilled each and every time I beat them because I knew I had beaten the best of the best.

Years later I was introduced to SPIN selling, which teaches you how to lead conversations with customers. A salesperson had to transition through four distinctly different types of questions: Situation, Problem, Implication, and Need/Payoff. Using the SPIN strategy, a salesperson gets a keener understanding of the customer's problems and needs and how to address them. PSS and SPIN professional sales training taught me a skill set that I continue to use and value to this day.

One particular concept I learned from SPIN sales training was calling on the right level of an organization, to make sure I "didn't take nos from people who can't say yes."

For example, many years ago, I was trying to sell a large amount of videoconferencing equipment (worth over $700,000) to Norfolk Southern Railroad. The company's IT staff had an interest in connecting their Atlanta, Norfolk, and Roanoke offices and put out a request for proposal (RFP) that my company and others responded to. Because my company was primarily selling telecommunications equipment in Memphis and Nashville, breaking into a remote market like Atlanta was a very big deal, and I felt the pressure to land the business or lose my job.

After we successfully demonstrated video connectivity between the three offices to the Norfolk Southern management team, I was convinced that the deal was ours. A few days later, I called the IT manager to get a status report and was informed that my biggest competitor was being awarded the contract. I was beyond stunned. I didn't know what to do next. Give up? No way.

So, I waited a few more days and called the IT manager back, only to be informed once again that the decision was made and my company would not be getting the business. I still couldn't believe his answer, so I decided that the third time would be the charm. I called him back—and got the same response as before.

I decided enough was enough. "I worked really hard to earn your business and respectfully refuse to accept your answer," I said. The IT manager went ballistic. Being told no three times was intimidating, but I remembered what I had learned in my sales training: I decided not to take nos from a person I wasn't 100 percent sure would or could ever say yes. I had to see if there was any way I could save the business.

A few days later, I found another contact in the purchasing department at Norfolk Southern who was happy to discuss the project and provided valuable information about their decision-making criteria. Once we received that information, we proceeded to conduct another demonstration for the IT manager and his team, which went very well. Not long afterwards, I was informed that my company was being awarded the contract for the project. Great news! And none of this would have happened if I had given up and taken a no from someone who really couldn't say yes.

This is just one of the simple concepts that helped me close millions of dollars of business in my sales career. It was also a concept that translated to my success as an entrepreneur.

Sales Is an Art That Requires Relationships

Sales, like entrepreneurship, is both an art and a science, and for both, the art is most evident in the area of personal relationships. Here's a real-life story of old-school selling tactics I recently used to position our company for a very large project at the University of Memphis. Ironically, even though I am a significant donor and active alum, my company had done very little AV work for the university in the past decade. Instead, they had consistently chosen our biggest competitor, which I found frustrating, to say the least. Since we understood that our competition had a long-term relationship with the customer and the inside track on future projects and opportunities, to even throw our hat in the ring meant we definitely had our work cut out for us.

We knew we needed to call on certain people in key positions at the university to tell them our story and hopefully further our cause. How did our salesperson initially try to accomplish that? You guessed it: he sent an email and then followed up many weeks later with a calendar invite from Outlook. After many more weeks, what kind of response do you think he got? Nothing. The potential client went quiet and didn't respond to any of the emails, texts, or voice mail messages. What did our salesman do about it? He basically just threw up his hands and said that the client was rude for not responding to him. He essentially gave up.

As a professional salesman, that response was simply not acceptable to me. I decided to try a different tactic by going old school. I ignored the fact that I didn't have an appointment and instead focused on making something happen with the account. I drove to the client's office unannounced and approached him as he was walking out of a meeting. Old-fashioned face-to-face communication: what a novel idea.

What happened next? Not only was the client highly receptive to discussing the upcoming project with me, but he also went on to identify several additional opportunities around the campus that could generate even more business for us. How did this happen? We decided not to let technology deter us from our mission and persevered in doing what we had to do to connect with the client one-on-one. Although I wouldn't recommend showing up without an appointment as an everyday sales tactic, the truth was, the old-school way *worked*. Based on that meeting, we were optimistic about securing a lot of business from the university in the future.

That's why I believe sales is not only a crucial skill set for an entrepreneur, but it's also a noble profession in and of itself. Historically, America has produced the best salespeople in the world, from Zig Ziglar to Jack Welch to Steve Jobs. I can't help but wonder: where is the next generation of super salespeople? Unfortunately, as I observe the current state of sales in so many industries, I see both the science and the art of sales slipping.

First, we're valuing sales training less and less. Although many top executives began their careers in sales, many of them mistakenly believe their salespeople possess the same skills they possess and ignore the need for training. At its zenith, Xerox put new hires through months of sales training before they ever called on a customer. In the computer, insurance, real estate, chemical, automobile, software, furniture, appliance, security, and many other industries, superb sales skills are critical for career success. Yet, the sales training curriculums that built these companies (and in some cases, the companies themselves) have virtually disappeared. Sadly, I have observed that many business owners and sales managers of today view sales training programs like PSS and SPIN as relics of the past, not relevant in today's marketplace.

Why? Many believe that technology is the answer to everything in sales, advising salespeople to send a text or email rather than meeting with the customer and engaging them in person. It's easier for everyone, right? Yes, sales is a set of techniques, but it is also an art, and it is the art of sales that is lost when we shortcut the process. Put simply, it's a flawed strategy. Today I see too many salespeople taking a strictly reactive role, simply answering their phones and becoming, in essence, order takers. Is that really selling? In my opinion, too many salespeople in too many companies are using technology to do their selling for them. For so many businesses, selling has become a series of emails, texts, and tweets, and in-person selling has become a thing of the past.

For the record, as a thirty-plus-year veteran of the videoconferencing industry, I do value the role of technology in the sales process. I also understand that selling is vastly different these days; thanks to the internet, today's buyer is nearly 60 percent along the purchase pathway before their first contact with sales. Social selling tools like LinkedIn continually feed prospects and customers valuable information to help them with their purchase decision, make them aware of new trends, and alert them of disruptive topics in their industry. Other technology tools like Customer Relationship Management (CRM) programs can be of great assistance in retaining valuable customer information, managing a sales funnel, and much more.

Social selling tools can also help salespeople use their prospecting time more efficiently and, therefore, more effectively. The better prepared you are before you contact your customer, the better your chances to make the sale. Using social selling tools to build knowledge about your prospects means much of the salesperson's work can be done in advance.

However, as helpful as all these tools can be, sales is still sales, and people still buy from people. It is important to acknowledge that technology should not be the primary means of communication with the customer. I'm reminded of the old saying that videoconferencing allows people "to do everything face-to-face except shake hands," and to me that means technology is one of many tools in the sales process, but it is not the process itself.

And like any other tool in the sales process, technology should be used judiciously. Whether it's selling copiers in the past or technology equipment today, nothing can replace communicating in person. How else can you really get to know your customers and their interests? Recognize buying signals? Build a relationship? Those issues can only be understood when meeting in the flesh. Many times, the best place to meet is in the customer's office, not only for their convenience but to provide an opportunity to build a relationship. I have lost count of the times I have built priceless customer rapport by simply meeting in their office in person. By meeting in the customer's office, I got the chance to know them better by checking out pictures, plaques, and memorabilia on their wall or desk. At a glance, you know what interests them, who their favorite sports teams are, and their hobbies. It is a priceless opportunity to see the customer as a person. Frankly, you can't point and click to build this kind of rapport. I'll say it again: I can only speak for the tech industry, but too often, salespeople want to hide behind technology and let emails, texts, or social media do their selling for them.

One of the most exciting technologies developed in the past thirty years is videoconferencing—such a great way to cost effectively connect with people all around the world. On many levels, videoconferencing makes sense for companies, schools, and hospitals who need to provide remote virtual access. Of course, technology has its limitations. And the truth is, there are some things you just don't do through a videoconference. For instance, you don't fire someone on a videoconference; it's just not professional. And from a sales perspective, you also don't sign contracts and close business on a videoconference. Sales is more of a high-touch process, which means you need to look a customer in the eye when negotiating a deal or working out a business issue. A caveat to this is if you're running a virtual-only business; in that case, videoconferencing is certainly an improvement over voice-to-voice. Also, if you run a small, niche business where a good percentage of your prospects live thousands of miles away, visiting every prospect in person likely wouldn't be cost effective. However, even in these cases, if you want to engage in high-value sales, I'd recommend you find a way to meet to face-to-face, whether you fly out to meet with your highest value prospects, attend in-person conferences for lead generation, or plan a site visit at some point during the project.

Whether it's 1978 or 2020, I truly believe sales is an honorable profession and continues to be a great way to make a living. I also have to agree that technology, such as social media, has an important place in today's sales process, particularly in promoting new products and services. But based on my experience, person-to-person meetings are still a key ingredient in achieving sales success and building strong, lasting business relationships. They're also where professional salespeople can leverage their sales skills to win accounts, advance their careers, and ultimately build the long-term value of the business. Relationships are the cornerstone of a business's value, both tangible and intangible. It's hard to build that value through texts, tweets, or emails alone.

Swing for the Fences

- Sales is an honorable profession that deserves respect; thriving sales equals a thriving business.
- Professional sales is both an art and a science; training your salespeople is always a good investment.
- Technology is an important tool in the sales process, but it shouldn't be the primary method of communication with the customer or prospect.
- Meeting customers face-to-face is still vitally important in building long-term business relationships and increasing the long-term value of the company.

Chapter 6
Don't Burn Bridges

People burn their bridges until they realize they're stranded . . . and then it's too late.

—Anonymous

In the early 1990s, I was working for a local telecom company as a data products manager. In five years, I built its videoconferencing division from zero to five million dollars. We were really flying high—that is, until the company decided to fire me right before Christmas on my thirty-ninth birthday. The telecommunications business was going through some major upheaval at the time, and the decision was made to have the company focus on selling its core products rather than videoconferencing systems. It was a humiliating experience that not only angered me but put my family in a helluva bind.

I don't deserve this, I thought. *Hadn't I built a five-million-dollar business out of nothing in five years? I put my blood, sweat, and tears into building a department the company could be proud of. And this is how they treat me?*

I was beyond angry and had every right to be. To make matters more interesting, since I was considered the subject matter expert on videoconferencing, some of my former co-workers and managers called to ask questions about equipment after I left. At first I was flabbergasted. *How dare they fire me and then call me to ask for my help? What audacity!* But after taking a few deep breaths, I had a decision to make: Did it make sense to carry a grudge against my old company? Should I badmouth them and sever ties? Was that the smartest thing to do? Or would I take a different and perhaps more difficult route?

After many days of soul searching, I finally made the choice to continue to take phone calls from my former co-workers and managers. I freely gave them information on hardware, networks, and competitive equipment to help them out. And I'm not going to lie; it was painful at times. But I also have to admit, I found it flattering that my former company was coming to me for my help. And I also had to acknowledge that I felt that much better for having taken the high road to reconcile with my former employer and protect my reputation.

Interestingly, as time went on, my former co-workers made it a point to return the favor by supplying me sales leads and market intelligence, which helped me get my new business (ISI) off the ground. The result of my choice was amazing. Those leads helped ISI grow significantly through the years by producing many thousands of dollars in new sales revenue. Things work out better when you don't hold a grudge.

The Quickest Way to Devalue Your Business

Fast forward to the summer of 2007 when four key members of my sales team (who represented 80 percent of the company's 2006 revenue) left the company. One after another they walked out the door.

It was devastating. And it all happened in just a little over thirty days. I remember feeling that ISI was a house of cards quickly collapsing and there was nothing I could do about it. At the time, I took the turnover personally and was angry at my ex-employees who had put me and ISI in such a serious bind.

For the record, one of my ex-employees decided to work for one of our major suppliers; another started his own company, which supplied streaming video and recording devices; and still another left to go to work for an ISI customer. As fate would have it, my newly formed sales team and I bumped into several of my ex-employees time and time again—awkward, for sure. But what do you do about it? How long do you hold a grudge? And is anger really a management strategy? Was there another way to look at the issue?

Although it took some time to process everything, in the end, we took a more positive approach, and I'm so glad we did. Instead of holding a grudge, we stayed connected and viewed our ex-employees as potential resources for helping ISI grow. Ironically, in the past ten years, ISI has collaborated on numerous accounts and business opportunities with our ex-employees, resulting in significant business revenue—all because we chose to put our feelings aside and do what was best for the business.

If you're like me, through the years you've heard this saying fairly consistently: "Don't burn bridges."

If you haven't heard this saying before, let me break it down for you. Burning bridges basically means you're ending a professional or even personal relationship in such a way that it cannot be rectified. Based on both my personal and professional experience, you never want to put yourself in a position where you've tarnished a connection, destroyed a professional relationship, or burned a co-worker (figuratively or literally).It just doesn't make sense. And on the practical side, there is no faster way to lower the value of your business to potential acquirers than to leave behind scorched earth.

Your Reputation Is Your Biggest Asset

First of all, for better or worse, the business world is all intertwined. One bad experience can follow you from career to career, office to office, and position to position.

This includes the way you deal with customers. Though they rarely give praise after a good experience with a company, unfortunately, customers tend to spread the word when they have a bad experience. With critical reviews, you develop a reputation with your customer and your industry—and it won't be a good one. Developing a bad reputation with customers can potentially harm professional opportunities as well as career earnings potential. It's important to recognize that no matter where you are and what you're doing, it really is a big, small world, and you need to protect your reputation and good name—no matter what. At the end of the day, when you leave this world, the most important legacy you leave is your reputation. For that reason alone, you should avoid burning bridges at all costs.

In addition, it is very difficult to make a decision about the value of a relationship (business or personal) because whatever decision you make, you have to live with it for a long time. By burning a bridge to your past, you're mortgaging the future. You might feel better in the short term, but what about the long term? Is that the best attitude to have? Isn't there a more productive way to deal with strained relationships?

One of the most important lessons I have learned in my career is that you never know where people will end up in the future and when your paths may cross again. In today's world, people tend to change jobs and companies much more frequently than in the past. People might change jobs a dozen times before they retire. So it's important to be careful to protect not only your professional reputation but your personal one as well. Remember the old saying, "What goes around comes around." And there is also a practical side to that mentality that can be monetized as well.

Even Your Ex-Customers Are Valuable

Instead of burning bridges, once the bridges are built, always take the high road. It may be steeper, but it gives you a distinct advantage. Regardless of your industry, the business world is all about doing business, and you want to be the one who makes things happen rather than the one putting up obstacles by being defensive or petty. Even if you disagree with your business partners and potential clients or if people abuse your trust or if you just don't get what you want, taking the high road ensures that you'll earn people's respect instead of their hatred or spite. This means responding professionally to others' opinions and actions with the utmost tact, consciously considering other points of view and never retaliating.

Through the years, I have lost count of how many times ISI would have a dozen or so reasons to sever a relationship with a customer but, in the end, chose not to do so. In many cases, it was not the easiest thing to do, and we often agonized about it. In some cases, the customers' treatment of us bordered on abuse. And frankly, as the company owner, I had to decide when enough was enough and protect my employees and our reputation. In those cases, we had every reason to fire the customer and move on. But instead of taking the easy way out and giving in to anger and frustration, we took a deep breath and decided to take the high road with our ex-customers and play the long game. We came to the conclusion that it was far more important to focus on the future than the past. And as tough as it was, we made a conscious decision to continue to keep it professional and make ourselves available to our ex-customers by providing whatever assistance they needed, even after they cut ties with us.

That's when we learned that our ex-customers could still be valuable. Exactly who were our ex-customers? We defined ex-customers as companies and organizations who had bought something from ISI at one time or the other but had chosen (for whatever reasons) not to continue to do so. And when we really thought about it, our ex-customers didn't just pay for our products and services at one time; they also had the ability to provide valuable word of mouth referrals to prospective customers. So, while you may not be able to monetize a customer who no longer does business with you, they may still play a critical role in influencing others who are looking to buy from you. Word of mouth is a powerful sales strategy. By treating your ex-customers with honor and respect, you are likely to retain their goodwill, which will go a long way in bringing new customers to your business.

Plus, ex-customers can always return. A customer could end a partnership for a variety of reasons. They may no longer have a need for your product or service, or they may get sideways with a sales or support representative. Other times, they may be lured by cheaper quotes from your competitors. However, none of these indicate a permanent departure, and by extending goodwill to ex-customers or ex-prospects, you keep the door open for their return. At ISI we called this the "boomerang effect" when a customer tried another vendor but eventually came back to do business with us. I can remember a private school in Tennessee who did that very thing. After many years and a lot of hard work on our part, which included working around the clock during the Christmas holidays, they chose to sever the relationship. ISI had every reason to be incensed. We didn't deserve this kind of treatment. Should we burn bridges with this customer? Retaliate? That would have been the easy way out. Instead, we decided to patiently wait for another opportunity to work with the client in the future.

Three years after the customer severed ties with ISI, the boomerang came back, and we ended up getting involved with several of the customer's new projects, which resulted in booking over five million in business. Pretty crazy, huh? How did that happen? Were we just lucky? Could be. But maybe it's because we chose to take the high road rather than burn bridges.

Another example of the boomerang effect was in the early days of ISI when we were still trying to get the business off the ground. A large local healthcare institution was interested in purchasing a number of videoconferencing systems from us. After many months of demonstrations and meetings with the manufacturer (including a trip to Virginia that ISI paid for), we felt like ISI had worked really hard and was well positioned to win the business.

On the day we were sure they would issue a purchase order to us, we were abruptly informed that they made the decision to buy the equipment from our competitor, another large telecom provider. I was stunned. And truthfully, I didn't really know how to react. Their response was not only shocking but also totally unexpected and couldn't have come at a worse time. ISI was still in the startup phase and needed to bring in a big order to turn the corner and become profitable. It was a certainly a bitter pill to swallow, but we quickly realized we couldn't let their decision ruin ISI's whole year. And as painful as it was, we recognized that we had a job to do, which was to move on and continue to grow the company.

And then a funny thing happened. A little over a year after ISI lost the sale, we got a call from that same healthcare institution. The other company had done a poor job with the videoconferencing project implementation, and they desperately needed help—now. Was I surprised by the call? Not really since I knew that they should have chosen ISI from the get-go. But since I am only human, I have to admit that I got a chuckle out of it as I thought, *I told you so.*

I quickly realized this was no time to hold a grudge. Instead, I worked to provide them new equipment. And the funny thing was, once I submitted my cost proposals, they never challenged our pricing. Pretty amazing, right? I had to wonder if they felt a little guilty for what happened the previous year. To this day, I'm not 100 percent sure, but I do know that by taking the high road and not burning bridges, ISI was able to secure a major client who was a highly profitable account for many years.

Sometimes, as a business owner, you have to set aside personal disappointments and grudges to do what's right for the company. Many times it's wise to pause and look at the issues from a different perspective. And don't underestimate the benefit of leveraging past relationships to help the company. Back in 2007 when we made the decision to reconnect with several ex-ISI employees who had abruptly left that summer, one of my team members reminded me that my ex-employees went to work for companies that were supplying both key products as well as sales leads to ISI. In other words, they represented value to the company. He said, "Think about this: you'll have the benefit of those two guys working for you without having them on the company payroll." It was a new way of looking at the situation from a less emotional perspective, and when I stopped and thought about it, he was right. There was no point to burning bridges with our ex-employees, though it was tempting to do so. By setting aside personal feelings and focusing on the future, it became a win-win proposition for both ISI and our ex-employees.

When you stop and think about it, life is way too short to hold a grudge. And that applies not only to your employees but to customers and suppliers—even family members and friends—as well. This philosophy makes so much sense to me and has paid personal and professional dividends.

Swing for the Fences

- Never burn bridges. Make this principle part of your company culture and reinforce this strategy with your employees.
- Remember the long-term business benefits of maintaining amiable relationships with not only ex-employees but customers, business partners, and other industry professionals as well.

- Taking the high road can have a positive impact on your brand. It never pays to hold a grudge in your business or personal life.
- Anger is not a management strategy, so avoid making long-term decisions based on short-term emotions.
- You never know where people will end up in the future, so it never pays to burn bridges.

Chapter 7
Employee Loyalty and Company Culture

Corporate culture is the only sustainable competitive advantage
that is completely within the control of the entrepreneur.
—David Cummings

Through the years I have always been proud of ISI's sales success. But to this day, I take even more pride in our incredible employee loyalty. For twenty-plus years, ISI had many employees who had been with the company for five, ten, fifteen, and even twenty years. On top of that, for several years, ISI had zero turnover, which is totally unheard of in the business world.

When compared to other companies our size, ISI's rate of retention and lack of employee turnover was astounding. So, how *did* we keep our people for so long? Was it my winning personality? Or did we do some things at ISI that other small businesses simply chose not to do?

Well, it didn't happen by accident. As my wife Maureen often said to me, one of the perks of running your own business is that you can run it any way you want, even if it's not in the corporate handbook. Looking back, ISI's employee strategy can be boiled down to a pretty simple formula: lead from the heart, provide competitive compensation, and offer meaningful work.

Lead from the Heart

First of all, from day one, we always treated employees like family. It began with simple things, like making it a point to know the names of employees' spouses, children, and/or significant others. But over time it went much further than that. Even with fifty-plus employees, we were a close-knit group who always had each other's backs. Why did we behave like that? Because that's what families do. It was part of our brand, and our current and prospective employees understood that. At ISI we didn't just talk the talk, we walked the walk. And as the CEO, every day I was in the office I made it a point to lead with my heart.

Several years ago, our accounts payable manager received an unexpected and serious cancer diagnosis. It was tough news to process and shocking for both me and my employees. As fate would have it, the cancer was so serious it looked like our employee was going to be out for many, many months undergoing chemotherapy and various other treatments. It would be a difficult situation for all of us but particularly for my employee who wanted and needed to work to make ends meet. With her husband making a meager living as a farmer, she simply couldn't go without a regular paycheck from ISI.

So we contacted our HR consulting firm, who understood our dilemma and was generally sympathetic to the situation. But ultimately, they said business was business and recommended ISI pay our AP manager for her vacation and sick pay only, which amounted to around a month's worth of pay; she should be cut off after that. They made the point (legitimately) that if ISI did anything more, it would open the door for other ISI employees to request the same treatment, which could end up being very costly.

It was a tough problem with no easy answers, and I spent many sleepless nights weighing the pros and cons of my decision. I asked myself, *If you didn't want to take the advice of the HR professionals, then why did you sign up with them in the first place?* Weeks later, after many additional discussions and considerable soul searching, I finally made the decision to continue to pay our AP manager for as long as it took to get her back on her feet with a full recovery. Was it a magnanimous gesture on my part? Not really. We chose not to go with the HR firm's recommended course of action because it simply didn't feel like the right thing to do. Our AP manager had enough going on trying to deal with her diagnosis, and we didn't need to add money to her list of worries. Selfishly, I also have to confess that when I went to bed at night, I wanted to feel at peace knowing I did the right thing. In my opinion, any business, large or small, has to be about more than making money. A business has to have a conscience. As it turned out, our AP manager ended up being out for almost nine months, which made our decision costly indeed. But at the end of the day, I wanted us to walk the walk. We did that by supporting a loyal employee in her darkest hours. As a result, I was at peace, knowing I led with my heart.

Through the years, there were many more examples of leading from the heart, from sending baby presents to attending employees' parents' funerals to stopping by the hospital when an employee was dealing with healthcare issues. Though it sounds like common courtesy to treat your employees like human beings, it's amazing how many companies fail to pick up on this. In my career I have learned that it is important to demonstrate to your employees that you not only care about the work they do for you, but you also care about them and their families personally.

Many business owners struggle with creating a culture that encourages employee loyalty, but it's really not that complicated. Take care of your employees, and they will take care of you. And that's exactly what ISI employees did for me and the company each and every day.

Taking care of our employees didn't just include personal gestures. It also affected our company policy, which included allowing employees the flexibility to work from home to accommodate a particular personal or family need.

For example, one employee in ISI's purchasing department received some very tough news: her ten-year-old daughter was diagnosed with type 1 diabetes. I didn't know much about the condition at the time, but I learned it is a serious disease that requires constant attention and makes life particularly challenging. Since diabetes needs to be constantly monitored, someone had to be available most of the day should an issue arise. Given those circumstances, it was clear to me what ISI needed to do. I led with my heart and allowed our employee to work from home to support her daughter. Was it easy to have the company's procurement manager work remotely when we needed to have products purchased on a daily basis for critical jobs? Let me answer that: it was not. Some things ISI employees needed from our procurement manager could be handled by phone, but many others required a face-to-face discussion. It didn't take long to recognize that this arrangement was by no means ideal or convenient. But family came first at ISI, and we weren't looking for convenience or pats on the back for our decision. Again, it came down to doing the right thing. When you do the right thing, you send a clear message to your employees: we care.

Provide Competitive Compensation

As important as it is to lead from the heart, the truth is that employee motivation and longevity also depend on money. You can treat your employees like family, but if they don't believe they're being paid well enough for the work they do, it's hard to blame them if they don't stick around. Many employees regularly question if they are being fairly compensated. And from an employer's perspective, how much is enough? On one hand, just because a company pays its employees well, it doesn't guarantee that they will be with the company for the long haul. However, based on my twenty-plus years of experience, not properly compensating employees almost always creates turnover. So, what's the answer?

Providing competitive compensation shows your employees that you value them as workers and also as human beings. When people feel valued, they feel better about coming to work, and overall company morale tends to increase. And with strong company morale, employees are even more motivated to do a good job. Although money may not be a primary motivator for employees to remain with a company, it can be used to reinforce a company's culture. At ISI, that included periodically awarding performance bonus checks to an employee who went above and beyond in supporting our customers. We frequently awarded those bonuses in company-wide meetings so they could be recognized among their peers and all could see the company's appreciation for a job well done.

ISI also provided profit sharing benefits for several years as well as significant Christmas bonuses (one hundred dollars a year for every year they were with the company, for a maximum of twelve hundred dollars), which was greatly appreciated by the employees. One employee even made it a point to tell me how much he appreciated ISI's generous bonus instead of a ham or being enrolled in the Jelly of the Month club like in *Christmas Vacation*. For the record, yes, those bonuses did cost ISI a lot of money, and some years were more challenging than others to make the payout. But our employees never forgot what we did for them. That's what families are for, right? We let our considerate actions speak for us, which reinforced employee loyalty to ISI—and that was a good thing.

ISI also made a very big deal out of milestone employee anniversaries. We felt it was important to acknowledge the level of risk employees took on in choosing to work with a growing startup like ISI as opposed to working for a major corporation like IBM or FedEx. So, we gave employees a five-hundred-dollar check and a desk clock for their five-year anniversary. That simple gesture also nurtured pride and company loyalty. Employees who celebrated their ten-year anniversary or higher would receive a special dinner in their honor and a check for twenty-five hundred dollars. Or, in some cases, they were awarded travel certificates to take their family to Disney World, on a ski trip, or a cruise.

Without a doubt, my favorite recognition event was when ISI recognized the tenth anniversary of our vice president of operations. Instead of issuing a check or travel voucher, we decided to get creative. Since this employee was a golfing fanatic, we worked through our professional contacts to secure a ticket for him to attend the last day of the Masters in Augusta, Georgia. Getting a ticket to the Masters is really tough, period, but getting one for the last day when the champion is crowned is the experience of a lifetime. When I presented the Masters travel certificate to him, he was literally speechless and got really choked up. Truthfully, so did I. A grand gesture, sure, but it also sent a message to the other employees that in the tumultuous world that is the tech industry, ISI appreciated long-term loyalty and dedication.

Offer Meaningful Work

Certainly taking a personal interest in your employees and providing competitive compensation are important parts of creating a great company culture. But there is another important ingredient: giving your employees an opportunity to do meaningful work. Keep in mind that a strong and inspiring company culture gives employees a purpose for what they do. It connects your leadership team with the rest of the employees and binds them with a set of shared beliefs. Your employees want to feel like they are contributing to something larger than themselves. At ISI we executed that strategy by creating a culture of creativity and innovation where every employee had a voice. We constantly reinforced that if an employee—whether warehouse manager, receptionist, or salesman— had an idea, we wanted to hear about it. Unlike a big corporation with layers of bureaucracy, we consistently invited ISI employees to share ideas for new products and processes. It was that important to us. And our employees recognized that their opinion mattered to ISI and that they had an opportunity to make a difference. As we have observed for many years, creating a company culture that acknowledges employee's ideas and innovation goes a long way not only in retaining quality employees but in recruiting them as well.

The benefits of creating this kind of culture can be monetized in a number of ways beyond merely saving the expense of employee turnover. I remember several years ago when ISI was struggling to grow our telemedicine business and needed to come up with a competitive differentiator. In previous years, the company had done well selling the various telemedicine cart systems, clinical scopes, and tools. But the hardware marketplace was becoming increasingly cutthroat, which made it difficult to effectively compete. Also, customers were tending to view ISI's telemedicine products more like commodities, which meant everything was price driven. Those dynamics made it even that much more difficult to make a profit. That's when I turned to my team and asked for suggestions on how ISI could fix the problem. What do our telemedicine clients and prospects need? What is their biggest challenge?

After several meetings with the ISI sales and technical support teams, the recommendation was to create a whole new product no one else in the market had. That product was a remote monitoring tool called "ISI-Net," which allowed us to manage hundreds of telemedicine systems around the country and alerted us when there was an issue. It made perfect sense. ISI couldn't realistically afford to provide the necessary technical support for so many systems scattered across the entire country, so we put our heads together and decided to leverage technology to solve the problem.

After many months of collaboration, the ISI sales and technical support teams finally released the new product. What a great reaction we received from our clients and prospects. By giving our employees the latitude to create something new, we ended up redefining ISI's position in the telemedicine marketplace. Several months after the release of the product, ISI was awarded an $8.3 million-dollar project in Arkansas to provide statewide telemedicine systems. We were told by the customer afterwards that they were impressed by the capabilities and potential of ISI-Net. They also mentioned that by creating ISI-Net we had demonstrated that ISI was on the leading edge of innovation in the healthcare industry. We realized we were awarded the biggest contract in our company's history because we did something very simple: we listened to our employees. And I have to say that this common-sense strategy has paid major company dividends over the years.

The bottom line: if you want to boost employee loyalty *and* customer loyalty, you must create a work environment and culture people enjoy day in and day out. Looking back, I have to say we did just that at ISI. As we led from the heart, provided competitive compensation, and offered the opportunity for meaningful work, loyalty was a natural result.

Swing for the Fences

- Maintaining a strong company culture not only has a positive impact on employee retention but can also be used as a recruiting tool to attract new employees.
- Running any business, large or small, must be about more than just making money. A business has to have a conscience.
- Take care of your employees, and they will take care of you. It's really not that complicated.

- Provide meaningful work for your employees so they know they are contributing to something larger than themselves.

Being named a Top Workplace was such a big thrill for ISI, particularly because we were being recognized for our company culture and employee loyalty.

Chapter 8

Reinventing Your Business Before It's Too Late

Longevity in this business is about being able to reinvent yourself or invent the future.

—Satya Nadella, CEO, Microsoft

A successful company can never rest on its laurels. Being successful in the past doesn't guarantee success in the future. Over time companies have to be willing to adapt, evolve, and change. To succeed, many businesses need to periodically reinvent themselves to stay relevant and move forward. Throughout my career, I noticed that some of the world's most profitable companies achieved their track record of success by constantly reinventing themselves. And some didn't. Consider my former company Eastman Kodak. They dominated the color film market for many years only to fall prey to the emergence of digital photography, which they refused to embrace.

But some companies successfully reinvented themselves and followed a whole new trajectory. For instance, online retail giant Amazon started out as merely an online bookstore. Streaming service provider Netflix started off renting DVDs before they revolutionized the industry. These companies adapted with the times, evolving their products and strategies to stay at least one step ahead of their customers' needs. And in the world of technology, there is no better example of a company reinventing themselves than IBM.

When I was a junior in college, I had an opportunity to intern at IBM as a marketing support assistant. That one-year internship helped me recognize that I wanted to have a career in sales. Not only was working for IBM a great experience, but the pay wasn't bad either. I literally had money falling out of my pockets—not a bad situation for a struggling college student. The only downside was that I needed to drive an old station wagon because I had to haul around equipment, including correcting Selectric and memory typewriters. Though certainly not a car to attract young ladies, that old station wagon got the job done.

My desire for sales was almost killed one day when I was scheduled to install equipment in a federal prison. I have to admit I wasn't too excited about visiting the location, but if the company needed it done, then I was going to do it. Once I got to the prison, I struck up a conversation with the guy helping me unload the equipment. I asked if he worked for the warden.

"Oh, no, I'm a prisoner. And I swear to God, I didn't slit that lady's throat!"

When I heard that, I felt a little light-headed and wasn't sure how to respond, so I didn't. After gathering myself for a minute or two, I installed the equipment and provided user training, which took several hours. Those hours felt more like weeks to me. I couldn't wait to finish up and get the hell out of there.

Yet despite having that crazy experience, I've always made it a point to pay attention to the astounding success IBM has experienced through the years. Several years after I graduated college (1984), IBM was on top of the computing world, with its iconic personal computer (PC). IBM was successful because it didn't try to make and do everything itself and outsourced a lot of hardware components for their PCs to smaller manufacturers. The strategy was successful until it wasn't. That's when the "PC clones" (PCs built with cheaper components but running Windows) hit the market. This created a huge problem for IBM. And much like Eastman Kodak, the large and bureaucratic IBM was slow to respond and innovate, allowing countless number of smaller competitors to undercut its prices and severely impact company revenue. Sadly, in 1993, IBM posted an eight-billion-dollar loss, one of the largest losses in history for an American company.

IBM had faced a tough choice: would they innovate or cling to what had worked in the past? They decided to shift their business model and provide IT consulting and management services instead of focusing on building PCs. Because of this bold choice, by 2010, IBM saw serious growth. Part of their success came from the acquisition of over two hundred companies already servicing the IT sector. IBM also invested heavily in its server business. By 2013 they were the number one seller of enterprise server solutions in the world. Even now, IBM is regarded as a case study in successful corporate evolution. It's helpful to have such a role model as reinvention is the key to business survival, regardless of the size of the company.[4]

Another great example of a company reinventing itself is one I am personally familiar with. As I mentioned earlier, back in the early 1980s, I worked for Eastman Kodak selling high-end copier-duplicators. Our biggest competitor was Xerox. Founded as the Haloid Company (in 1906), Xerox got started manufacturing photographic paper. Ironically enough, both Xerox and Eastman Kodak were founded in Rochester,

New York, which made them crosstown rivals for many years. Over time, Xerox created the iconic xerographic process, which changed copier/duplicators forever and made the company a worldwide phenomenon. Yet after decades of success as a highly innovative company, Xerox experienced a serious downturn. How did that happen? As often happens in technology, rapid change occurred and Xerox simply was not prepared. On top of that, turmoil at their corporate offices in 2000 resulted in significant management failure. Xerox finally realized that things had to be reinvented in both their products and services. This was literally a do or die situation. Xerox saw that "what got you here won't get you there" and took the necessary steps to upgrade their technology.

Today Xerox sells a wide array of products, including toner, ink, software, scanners, inkjet printers, and copy machines and is an eleven-billion-dollar technology leader. Xerox has performed so well financially over the past several years that they are currently poised to make a major acquisition of tech giant Hewlett Packard, which will more than double the size of the company. Talk about a successful reinvention.

Some companies have to reinvent themselves after decades of success; others, like ISI, have to reinvent themselves just to get started. Back in 1996, selecting a videoconferencing product for ISI was much easier than it would be today. Only a handful of vendors (mostly US companies) dominated the marketplace, with very little to differentiate them. These same vendors already had resellers/integrators in place, which didn't bode well for a startup like ISI. Since we had built our business plan around providing industry-leading videoconferencing products, we were in a world of hurt and had to do something about it. So, at a very early stage, we reinvented ourselves to get the business off the ground. That was when an up-and-coming vendor approached us about selling their product, which was popular in Europe but had little presence in the US marketplace at the time. We thought, *What have we got to lose?*

Tandberg, based in Oslo, Norway, was revolutionizing the videoconferencing industry with products that were not only less than half the price of the competition but also very user friendly. Tandberg systems could easily connect on ISDN networks for dial-up video conferencing, which was poised for explosive growth in the future. It potentially looked like a good fit for the company, so ISI and Tandberg started the negotiating process in our office, which lasted until the late afternoon. I then told the Tandberg representative that I had a family matter to take care of and suggested we could wrap things up in the morning. The Tandberg representative was so excited about ISI becoming a reseller that he couldn't wait until the next day to meet. So, what did he do? He followed me to my son's Little League baseball game to continue our discussion and get the dealer agreement signed. Talk about persistence.

And it paid off for both companies. Over the next twenty years, ISI sold over fifty million dollars in Tandberg equipment and services and dramatically grew market niches like distance learning and telemedicine. ISI eventually became one of Tandberg's leading resellers in the United States. None of this would have happened had we not chosen to shift our strategy and reinvent our business plan. We took a chance on a product and company we felt had the potential to help us grow in the future. Looking back on it more than twenty years later, I am so glad we did.

Embrace New Products and Services

So how did we keep reinventing ourselves to stay profitable in such a volatile industry? One way was through embracing new products and services, making them part of the company's culture and go-to-market strategy.

Digital signage technology is a great example. We didn't initially offer it but recognized it was an emerging technology. And the more we thought about it, we realized that if ISI didn't provide digital signage, someone else would. Plus, many of our customers had multiple needs for the technology and were inquiring about it. For example, hospitals needed digital signage to provide directions for their patients and visitors, publicize events, advertise products, post appointment information, and more. A local children's hospital even had us install a video wall for their patients to access a wide variety of entertainment while waiting for their treatments.

Digital signage ended up being a hot market that has only continued to grow. Now museums, restaurants, hotels, and high-end retail locations enhance the customer experience with this technology. And that's the key. With digital signage, ISI leveraged state-of-the-art technology to help clients attract and retain more customers. And by embracing digital signage technology, ISI provided additional value to our customers and prospects, not only selling the hardware and software but also providing much-needed remote management services.

In fact, ISI leveraged digital signage technology to expand the company's service offerings into not just remote management but also managed IT services for clients. And besides selling the necessary digital signage hardware, which includes high-end LCD displays and video players, there is an even greater opportunity with digital signage, which is content creation. Having high quality content is extremely important to successful digital signage implementation because without it integrators are really just installing a fancy LCD display, which is no different than hanging another TV.

Whether you are in the tech industry or any other industry, a company must offer value beyond simply selling the latest "box." You must recognize this and develop a strategy that provides content to customers on an ongoing basis. Providing that content ends up being yet another way to create intellectual property and recurring revenue. And whether it's in the tech industry or any other industry, a company that has both intellectual property and recurring revenue will end up creating a lot more value than a company that doesn't have either one. Another benefit? Should there ever be a desire to someday sell the business, I can personally attest that potential acquirers *love* companies that have intellectual property and a steady source of recurring revenue.

The best part of all? Whether it's network and system design, end-user training, or content creation for digital signage applications, customers will pay for these services—and not just in the tech industry. Customers in any industry will pay for value-added services they cannot provide on their own. Not only will they pay for the services, but they will also pay more. The profit margins for services tend to be much higher than hardware.

Later, another opportunity presented itself in the form of streaming and recording video. Truthfully, at the time, we didn't know what it meant for ISI or for our customers. After additional investigation, we discovered that providing streaming video was not only a major market opportunity but also a technology of keen interest to our customers, one they were willing to make an investment in.

For example, instead of creating complicated systems for distance learning, ISI only needed to install one piece of equipment that could record classes and offer them through streaming video. And a major benefit of the technology was that the recordings could be archived and accessed remotely at any time of the day or night. This feature was particularly important for universities that wanted to provide on-going support to students who were unable to attend classes in person.

Although ISI enjoyed considerable success with selling audiovisual and videoconferencing products for many years, not every ISI product or service turned into gold. Several years ago, I was demonstrating a desktop video product to a major hospital in Memphis. When the management team assembled in the conference room and I hit the start button, puffs of smoke came out of the machine. Talk about embarrassing!

All I could think to say was, "Well, obviously we have a problem here." And after rescheduling the demonstration for a later date, I immediately shipped the malfunctioning equipment back to the manufacturer and received a replacement unit a short time later. I have to admit that when it was time for the do-over demonstration, my heart skipped a beat when I plugged the system in. But, all's well that ends well, and funny enough, once we were able to properly demonstrate the equipment, the customer bought several systems from us despite our less-than-stellar initial demonstration.

The takeaway? Don't be afraid to fail. Over the past twenty years, I have lost count of how many new products ISI introduced that not only didn't make us any money but also cost us valuable time (and money), including telecom systems, presentation equipment, holographic video, revolutionary new control equipment, specialized software, and more. But we were determined to grow the company and continue to reinvent ourselves, so we were willing to assume the potential risk. The truth is, you're not going to hit a home run with every product or service. That is just the way it is. But even if only one out of ten products you bring to market actually makes it, it's still worth it because if a business doesn't try to grow, it dies.

As a result, ISI lived and learned. As a company we remained focused on diversifying and reinventing ourselves to create a sustainable and profitable business model. Although ISI was entrenched in the tech industry, we wanted to present ISI as not just another AV/videoconferencing integration firm but as an emerging technology company. We wanted to be known as the company who was first to market with innovative, disruptive products and technology. We wanted our customers and prospects to look to us not just for the needs they had today but for the needs of tomorrow as well. From that standpoint, I believe we were highly successful.

Become a Service-Focused Organization

Another strategy that worked for us was transitioning to becoming a service-focused organization. For us, this included selling managed services, remote monitoring, maintenance, 24/7 support, and more.

To be honest, ISI recognized the opportunity for managing services way before other companies in the industry. How? We listened to our customers. For example, early on, major corporations and law firms contracted with ISI to provide support and monitoring for their video systems so that their employees didn't have to perform these functions. Besides being profitable, this service also increased customer satisfaction because our continuous monitoring of a customer's systems allowed us to solve technical problems in advance and fix glitches before they became a major problem. One contract that we secured from a major corporate client was initiated back in the early days of ISI (1999) and was renewed every year for twenty-plus years. Not too bad. And, once again, maintaining long-term, profitable relationships with customers not only increases the value of a business but also makes the company more attractive to potential acquirers.

So, what prompted ISI to start selling services when so many of our fellow integrators did not? It was an easy decision. We knew that if ISI didn't provide on-going service to our clients then we were opening the door for our competition to do so. And that simply made no sense. Also, even though service revenue in the tech industry tends to be a little lower than project-based/installation revenue, the profit margins are generally much higher. In fact, this is also the case in many other industries, like auto and home appliances. In these sectors, service and maintenance contracts provide a significant portion of total revenue.

However, for the record, selling services in the tech industry is not the same as selling products. It's a whole new ballgame. What you are really selling is an insurance policy of sorts. Given that fact, my initial advice to companies who are used to primarily selling hardware products is to hire a salesperson who does nothing but sell services all day, every day. My second piece of advice? Get creative in recruiting for this position by looking for people who may not have industry experience but do have a strong entrepreneurial mindset as well as great organizational and communication skills.

Several years ago, ISI hired a sales guy whose only previous experience was calling customers about overdue car payments, which, in many cases, resulted in repossessing their vehicles. Talk about a tough job. When we hired this individual, he told us how grateful he was about his new job at ISI since he didn't have to deal with customers who cussed him out or hung up on him (or both) on a daily basis. Truthfully, we weren't 100 percent sure how things would work out with this individual, but we had to try something new. The status quo wasn't cutting it, and ISI's services revenue numbers were flatlining.

For the record, I am not suggesting that focusing on selling service and maintenance contracts is a groundbreaking strategy. Far from it. But it was simply one of many ways we decided to get out of our comfort zone and embrace a new approach to grow our business. What is undeniable is that through this new product/service strategy, ISI was able to generate an additional twenty million dollars in revenue over the past twenty years. In the end, selling service and maintenance contracts was a key ingredient in taking the company to the next level. It also distinguished ISI from other competitors and greatly increased our industry visibility. And that, in turn, made the company that much more attractive to potential acquirers.

Listen to Your Customers

Many times, reinventing a company doesn't have to be agonizing and risky. How so? As noted earlier, ISI developed the simple strategy of listening to our customers when they had ideas. What better way to reinvent your business than to listen to the very people who are paying for your products and services and keeping you in business? And, truthfully, a customer you have a close relationship with also has a vested interest in the company's future success. Through the years, ISI was blessed to have a number of clients who fit that exact profile. We made it a point to listen to our customers on a regular basis, and they identified a number of additional support services the company could provide them.

One of those additional support areas was system and network design, which many companies simply didn't have the resources or knowledge to provide for themselves. It's no secret that the AV world is continuing to migrate to information technology (IT), which creates many complex issues, particularly in selecting a network configuration that works for both departments. Once the network was established, we learned it was also important for us to design the system hardware with the customer in mind. Translation: we needed to make sure that our systems were as user friendly as possible. And beyond providing the project design and installation, ISI also had an obligation to do user training on the systems.

User training proved to be a critical component as a newly installed AV (or any tech) system is essentially worthless if customers don't know how to use it. Common sense, right? Yet we were amazed to discover how many AV integrators completed an installation and either "fast tracked" the training on the system or didn't do it at all. Then they wondered later why their customers were irate. Truthfully, it wasn't that complicated; customers paid a lot of money for their AV systems and simply wanted to know how to use what they bought. Therefore, it is important for technology integrators (not just AV) to have a comprehensive, detailed training program that helps customers optimize their equipment, which, in turn, encourages maximum usage. And by the way, that includes hardware and software. Additional customer training opportunities technology integrators can provide include technical training for IT department staff and corporate administration personnel who, many times, need to know how to troubleshoot various technical problems that may arise from system usage.

Reinventing your company by embracing new products and services, growing the services business, and listening to customers are strategies that can work for any company in any industry. At the end of the day, big revenue is nice, but big profits are even better. Plus, a company focused on providing high-margin support services and intellectual property is also (once again) much more attractive to potential acquirers.

Swing for the Fences

- In today's hypercompetitive environment, a business needs to constantly look at reinventing itself to stay relevant.
- It's okay to fall in love with what you do but not with how you do it.
- Many of the best ideas for reinventing a business come from your customers, so listen to them.
- Businesses who are unwilling to change are destined to die.
- Reinventing any business is often a long and arduous process with many ups and downs.
- Any time you make a change in your business, be prepared for some setbacks along the way. Stay focused on the future and don't be afraid to fail.

Chapter 9

Customer Service Can
Make or Break Your Business

*A lot of people have fancy things to say about customer service,
but it's just a day-in, day-out, ongoing, never-ending, persevering,
compassionate kind of activity.*
   —Christopher McCormick, CEO, L.L. Bean

E arly one morning, my engineering manager stepped in my office and
closed the door.

"I've got an urgent matter I need to discuss with you," he said. "It
involves our biggest long-term customer."

Although I am not a morning person, that last part definitely got
my attention.

"What's the issue?" I asked. "How much trouble are we in?"

"If we don't go up to Paducah [Kentucky] this morning and fix a number of technical issues, we are in serious jeopardy of losing their business."

"Do what you have to do to make them happy," I responded. "I don't care how much time or money it takes."

That's all my engineering manager had to hear. He jumped in his car and made the four-hour trip to Paducah. When he got there, he addressed all of the customer's concerns and worked *all* night long to make sure everything was working properly prior to the big company meeting that next day. Even after that, with absolutely no sleep (he never even made it to the hotel), he stayed in the conference room on standby for the customer's peace of mind, should an issue arise.

Was this a one-time heroic gesture on ISI's part? Did we do it just because we thought we would lose the business? Absolutely not! From day one, providing superior customer service was in our company's DNA. It's what customers had come to expect from us, and it was part of the ISI brand. As I look back, I believe ISI's exceptional customer service was a key ingredient to the company's long-term success in the hyper-competitive world of technology. I realize I am beginning to sound like a broken record, but I do believe that ISI's reputation for outstanding customer service was just one more attribute that made the company attractive to potential acquirers.

I could share many more stories about how ISI went the extra mile to make a customer happy or meet a deadline. For instance, back in August 2005, we received an order for the installation of a large number of LED displays and related equipment for a very large casino in Biloxi, Mississippi.

Everyone at ISI was so excited about doing this project, not just because it was a cool venue but it was also a brand-new application for our technology that involved sophisticated video displays being installed in a newly featured lava lamp bar—pretty crazy and something

ISI hadn't done before. But our installation team was motivated and committed to meeting the challenge. On top of that, our customer mandated that the installation had to be completed before Christmas, which meant we had a little over four months to get the job completed. Not an easy task. And although it was a tight time frame, we understood that the deadline for the install was extremely important to the casino as they wanted to take full advantage of the holiday season to attract new customers. We were to begin the install in September, after Labor Day, and have it done on or before December 20th to give the casino plenty of time to get familiar with the equipment prior to Christmas. That was the plan. And then it wasn't.

If you're from the Gulf Coast area, you already know what happened right before Labor Day in 2005. Right as we were gearing up for the installation, Mother Nature had other plans. On August 23, 2005, Hurricane Katrina hit Biloxi and the Gulf Coast and ended up being one of the deadliest hurricanes to ever hit the United States.

The estimated death toll was over 1,833 people. Millions were left homeless, not only along the Mississippi Gulf Coast but in New Orleans as well. With that much devastation, the area would conservatively require many months and possibly years to rebuild, including the casino where ISI was scheduled to install equipment. Given all the devastation up and down the Gulf Coast, it looked like the project would be either delayed for an extended period or not happen at all.

Then in early October of 2005, we got the call—the one we never expected to receive in a million years. "The project is back on," our customer told us, "and it still needs to be completed before Christmas." We couldn't believe it. Did they just say that the casino expected to be fully operational a few months after one of the worst natural disasters to ever hit the United States? When we looked at the calendar after the call, we realized the project deadline was a mere 119 days after Katrina hit.

Complete a four-and-a-half-month installation project in less than three months? What's the old saying, "Pressure makes diamonds"? At the time, I thought their request sounded like insanity. I couldn't imagine we could pull it off. Candidly, the ISI operations team was more than a little concerned about both the crazy-tight time frames and the post-hurricane job site environment. We saw a number of big-time challenges, but as a company, we were also determined to support our customer to the best of our ability during an extraordinarily difficult time.

When the ISI team arrived in Biloxi, they quickly recognized that the installation environment was unlike any they had ever seen before. It was truly like working in a war zone, with no electricity, cell service, hotels, or restaurants. In fact, the nearest place to get a hotel room or something to eat was several hours away. With no electrical connections on the job site, the ISI team was forced to use generators to power their tools and other equipment. It was a surreal environment that looked like a scene from World War II. Everywhere they looked, they saw total devastation. But rather than complain about the difficult working conditions, our team stayed focused and worked incredibly hard to make the customer happy and complete the project on time.

It was a long, arduous installation that took many weeks to complete, and the ISI team gave it the maximum effort, working twelve to fourteen hours a day, seven days week, for over three months. It was an incredible effort, and we felt good about what we had accomplished. When the bar officially opened on Christmas Eve, the ISI ops team felt a tremendous sense of satisfaction, knowing the company had provided above-and-beyond customer service and had turned a total disaster into a wonderful success story.

Those are just two of the many successful customer service stories from ISI's twenty-plus year history. When you get down to it, what is customer service, really? Why was ISI so good at it when other companies were not? I can sum it up in two words: *we cared*. We didn't just talk the talk; we walked the walk and let our actions speak louder than our words. It wasn't rocket science. It was who we were.

Being surrounded by that level of customer service for over twenty years, I have to admit that I probably get more irritated than most when I experience poor customer service. In my opinion, the airline industry is one of the worst offenders. Why do I say that? Over the past several years, my wife and I have been scheduled on several flights that have been cancelled at the last minute for unknown reasons. One flight out of Chicago on a Sunday afternoon was delayed until Wednesday of the next week. Apparently, we were expected to pay for three days' worth of food and hotel expenses because the airlines decided at the last minute not to fly their plane. Needless to say, we received neither a reimbursement nor an explanation. I couldn't help but wonder, *Did anyone at the airlines ever think about how their customers would feel? Did they even care?*

With our flight cancelled, we had to rent a car (at our own expense) and drive the five-hundred-plus miles back to Memphis in snowy and icy conditions. The experience was nerve wracking, to say the least. Again, no compensation, apologies, or explanations given whatsoever.

Several other times, flights were delayed to the point of missing our necessary connections to get to important meetings, which ended up costing my wife and me hundreds of dollars in additional hotel and food expenses. What happened in these cases? You guessed it. The airline company did absolutely nothing to cover the cost of the hotel room. However, they did make a weak attempt at compensating us for our inconvenience by offering us dinner vouchers for eighteen dollars per person. Seriously? That amount would barely cover the cost of drinks.

Of course, it's not just the airline industry. More recently, my wife and I decided to put a new roof on our home in Florida. It was an older home, built in 1963, so it was time. We did our homework and identified a firm that had done a lot of work in our neighborhood and seemed to have a solid reputation. Once we signed the paperwork to authorize the work, we painstakingly went through all the details associated with completion and specifically reminded the company that they would need to pull a permit prior to any work being done. Also we specifically scheduled the work for a certain week in March so we could be there to oversee the install. We let the firm know all this more than two months in advance. From anyone's standpoint, that was more than enough time.

In March, on our way from the airport to our house, my wife and I got a call from the roofing company telling us they couldn't start work because they didn't have a permit. In fact, they couldn't even tell us when they could get it. To say we were upset is an understatement.

But it gets better. Once they finally pulled the permit and were ready to start the installation, my wife and I were informed that they had not received delivery of the tile for the roof. And then they started playing the blame game and pointed fingers at the manufacturer, who they claimed had fumbled the ball.

I couldn't believe it. *Really? You are blaming someone else for your problem?* And then I asked the project foreman, "Did anyone think about following up and calling the manufacturer to check the status of the delivery?" The project manager sheepishly admitted that they hadn't done that and then proceeded to try to convince me once again that it wasn't their fault, again putting the blame on the manufacturer.

At that point, I disclosed to the project manager that I had a lot of experience dealing with vendors in my own business and that fumbling the ball several times and then blaming someone else was totally unacceptable. My thoughts on the subject? When a customer purchases something from you, they have expectations, and companies need to work hard to meet those expectations. Thankfully, my wife and I did get the roof installed several weeks later, but as you can imagine, the whole experience left a bad taste in our mouths.

My point in sharing these stories isn't merely to complain. Think about the poor customer service you have received from companies. It's a good reminder that when customers put their trust in a company to deliver a product or service, the experience matters as much, if not more, than the final result. If a company misses details or doesn't think about possible inconveniences from the customer's perspective, even if you end up receiving what was promised, you're unlikely to do business with that company again unless you absolutely have to.

Also, because many companies *don't* focus on customer service, businesses that go the extra mile really stand out. That creates value not just for the customers but for the business as well. Take Amazon, for instance. Not only does Amazon have a wide selection of products to choose from, but the experience of doing business with them is also good for the customer. Think about it. As an Amazon customer, after you find what you want, you can make the purchase with one click. What could be easier? Once the order is placed, Amazon takes care of their customers by emailing order confirmations as well as up-to-the-minute shipping information. That's the key to providing good customer service; many times it's not the grand gestures but a series of little things that ultimately makes the difference.

In any business, things can go wrong. In the event that an Amazon shipment is received and ends up being the wrong size, color, etc., you can arrange for a quick return through the website where you can even print the necessary shipping label to make the process as painless as possible. At the end of the day, by any measure, Amazon has grown to be a highly successful company over the past several years, with many billions of dollars in sales. I am sure many factors have contributed to their success, but in my opinion, the number one reason is their exceptional customer service.

Another example is FedEx. Besides providing guaranteed overnight delivery of a package, what are they really selling? In my opinion, they are selling peace of mind. Their whole process has been developed with the customer in mind. Not only can you rest assured that once you drop off a package it will be delivered on time, but you also have up-to-the-minute online access to the status of delivery. In other words, they provide all the information customers need to make the experience of dealing with FedEx a positive one. So, as with Amazon, it's not about heroic, grand gestures for customers, but little day-to-day things that add up to a happy and, oftentimes, long-term customer.

What about customer service in your industry? Can you think of companies that really go the extra mile in serving their customers? What would it take to go that extra mile in your own business? In recent years, AV has survived the tech boom by essentially merging with the IT industry. That has not only demanded new skills from AV professionals but has also forced the industry into a more consultative role, rather than being a project-to-project machine. This has made the end-user experience all the more important. Rather than focusing on displaying flashy new technology solutions to clients, now more than ever companies need to focus on the customer service behind the tech.

Here's the bottom line: those stories about how ISI showed up for our customer in Kentucky and Biloxi weren't a series of one off's that made for good story telling. They were examples of the way we did business all day every day because we cared about our customers and our reputation. And for the record, providing exceptional customer service results in a great return on your investment, not just in technology but in any industry. Here are ten good reasons a company must focus on customer service:

1. No matter what industry you are in, it is always cheaper to keep an existing customer than to find a new one. In fact, providing good customer service can lead to an increase in

customer retention that equates to an increase in the company's net income.

2. Customer service represents your company's brand image, mission, and values. Today's customers and prospects many times make assumptions based on a company's social media presence, product advertisements, and other external marketing. A company's customer service team, however, is the strongest connection to their customers because they are representing your company's brand.

3. It is important in any industry to have motivated customer service employees because they will, in turn, make it their mission to create satisfied customers. No matter what industry you are in, no employee is going to enjoy coming to work if they are treated poorly, particularly compared to other company employees. That is why it is so important for a business to take care of their customer service team.

4. Satisfied customers not only buy from your company but can also be a great source of additional business by providing references to prospects. When customers are happy, they are far more likely to spread the word and share their positive experience with other business associates and friends. Also, as noted above, the happier your customer service team is, the greater the likelihood they will work even harder to satisfy and exceed your customer's expectations.

5. In any industry, good customer service encourages customers to remain loyal to your company. When a customer has a positive experience with your company's brand, they have no reason to look elsewhere.

6. Customers in any industry are willing to pay more to companies who offer better customer service. It matters so much that they would rather deal with a company they feel safe with than go

price shopping. And truth be known, customers many times will make purchase decisions based on their experiences with the service department, not the sales department. In today's business environment, many companies are working hard to prioritize customer service because they recognize that any company that doesn't do so will crash and burn.

7. Customer service employees can offer important insights and feedback about customer experiences because what matters most is how your customer perceives your brand. In fact, many customers are more likely to confide in their customer service representative than their sales representative. Also, with a solid, motivated customer service team, your company's brand can stay ahead of changing customer interests and needs, which is particularly important in the tech industry.

8. Providing good customer service has the potential for growing a customer for life, which translates into the revenue a company can expect from a single customer account. Making an investment in your customer service department is a great way to cultivate a customer for life. The more customers for life a company is able to retain, the more value a business has to a potential acquirer.

9. Too often, companies simply react to customer service problems rather than taking steps to prevent them. It is important for a company to be proactive in handling customer service issues. Besides getting ahead of potential customer problems, a company with a proactive customer service department also creates marketing opportunities to measure customer satisfaction. It also sends a message to the marketplace that your company is forward thinking and really values customer relationships. Proactive customer service is also a unique and effective marketing tool for companies introducing and

promoting new products and services and has the added benefit of augmenting the efforts of the company sales team.

10. No matter what industry you're in, you want your business to stand out, and a great way to do that is to provide exceptional customer service. It can be a powerful competitive advantage and an excellent differentiator for your company. In addition, continuing to provide excellent customer service is also a great way to retain customers and attract new ones.

At ISI, we took above-and-beyond service to a new level in our industry. We simply provided a level of customer service that our competition either couldn't or chose not to. For over twenty years, over 90 percent of ISI's annual revenue was earned from repeat customers. Why? Because they were happy with our performance. Our employees also knew that providing exceptional customer service wasn't just a nice thing to do occasionally. It was our day-to-day lifeline for keeping the company solvent, promoting growth, and eventually becoming attractive to potential acquirers.

Swing for the Fences

- Providing good customer service is essential for any business to succeed. Not providing it almost always means failure.
- Customers are willing to pay more to companies who offer better customer service.
- In many industries, customer service revenue is by far a company's most profitable source of revenue. It also has the potential to create customers for life.
- Having a solid reputation for providing good customer service is not only a competitive advantage but also tends to increase the value of a company to potential acquirers.

Chapter 10
Passing the Torch

Succession planning helps build the bench strength of an organization to insure its long-term health, growth, and stability.
—Teala Wilson

Over the years, I have experienced many personal and professional challenges as an entrepreneur. I've mentioned several already, like the first year when financing issues almost put us out of business before we got a chance to get started. Then there was the little matter of my cancer diagnosis (melanoma) when I literally thought I was going to die and never see my business get off the ground. And if that wasn't enough, we closed the year out with a supplier who embezzled over fifteen thousand dollars. Looking back, it might have been the most challenging year I had ever been through, at least up to that time.

Little did I know more challenges were to come. Over the next several years we had to deal with a number of formidable obstacles, such as a nasty business divorce (1998), employee embezzlement of over $260,000 (2003), 80 percent employee turnover, and the death of a key employee (2007). Those last two events happened within thirty days of each other. At one point during that period, I thought I was losing my mind. Things were so bad I didn't want to turn the lights off in my bedroom at night because I was afraid of what the next day would look like. Those were a few of the many issues we had to deal with in building ISI into a successful company. I can also say unequivocally that there was never a dull moment.

Perhaps because of all those challenges and obstacles, ISI became more than just a company to me. It was my life's worth and professional legacy. It was never just business to me; it was always personal. ISI was my baby, and I was proud of what we had built through the years. I couldn't imagine anybody but me running my company. The very thought of succession planning was beyond frightening, which was why I avoided dealing with the issue for many years. My approach was, if I don't think about it, then maybe it will just go away. But eventually I realized that doing nothing wasn't a good option and presented a bigger risk for the future of the business. Doing nothing was really taking the easy way out of a difficult situation, and I have never been that kind of person. It was time for me to step up.

I finally realized I could no longer avoid addressing the succession issue for the sake of my family, my employees, and my customers. No matter how tough it was on me personally, I had to paint a picture of where ISI was going in the future. It was the least I could do. So, I researched best practices for succession planning in a small business.

First off, what is succession planning, exactly? In simple terms, succession planning is the process of passing control of the business to others. It involves creating a plan for someone to either own or run your business after you retire, become disabled, or die. Since one or more of these scenarios will eventually happen to everyone, succession planning is just common sense.

However, I had another reason to consider succession planning— one that was hard for me to admit. The pace of change in the technology industry was becoming overwhelming. In 2016, after twenty years in the business, I was going through a period of soul searching where I was asking myself some tough questions: *Have I lost my touch? Am I burned out? Am I getting too old to do this job?* And the big one that kept buzzing around in my head was, *Would the company be better off if I wasn't running it?*

Those were gut-wrenching questions that needed honest answers. Then an old saying came to mind: "you can fool some people some of the time, but you can't fool all the people all the time." I didn't want to fool myself. Struggling with these questions became part of my daily routine, and to be honest, it wasn't a good thing. As I mentioned before, when you're running a business, doubt can be a nasty enemy.

Finally, after many months of soul searching, I gained clarity. I had to admit to myself that, more and more, selling technology was a young person's business. The tech industry was simply moving too fast for me, and I was no longer interested in keeping up. I felt like I was losing my effectiveness, that my time had come and gone. I decided it was in the best interest of the company, my employees, and my customers to bring in a new, younger voice to lead them into the future.

Ironically enough, in 2015, as I was trying to plot the company's future (and mine), ISI received our first written offer to buy the company. Even though we had never expressed interest in selling, even during the flurry of offers when we made the *Inc.* 500 list in 2001, it turned out several companies in our industry wanted to expand into Tennessee, making ISI a likely target. I remember getting the call on my cell one day as I was headed out of the office. The caller identified herself and then immediately stated, "I know a lot about ISI, and I want to buy your company." To say I was a shocked would be an understatement. Truthfully, I wasn't sure how to respond.

After gathering myself, I responded that ISI wasn't for sale, but I would be happy to have further discussion about her interest. This company had been to our office months before and were first-class professionals with a great track record and industry reputation. So, as you can imagine, we were flattered to have an industry leader interested in buying ISI. We were also curious about the M&A process, so we moved to the next steps, which included both parties visiting each other's offices and having more detailed discussions about what an offer would look like. As a side note, a lot of these discussions were going on a few months before Christmas.

As you can imagine, there was a lot of back and forth between both companies and things got intense. Finally, a short time after Christmas in 2014, we received their offer. It was the first time ISI had received in writing an offer to purchase. Although the dollar amount was far below what we thought ISI was worth, we were, nonetheless, flattered to receive it. But after thinking through it, and acknowledging that offer was tempting, we decided to decline their offer. The timing wasn't right and the offer was too low, so we moved on.

Looking back on it, going through this process was far from a waste of time because it provided real-life experience with M&A that we were able to draw on several years later. We also got a keener understanding of what companies were looking for in a potential acquisition. After it was all said and done, the experience did serve another important purpose. With a written offer in hand from the potential acquirer, I had a benchmark to gauge the future value of the company and more clarity about what I wanted ISI's future to look like. As I thought about it further, I realized I wasn't personally ready to sell the company. Why did I feel that way? At the time, I felt ISI still had some gas in the engine and that our best days were in front of us.

So, after declining the offer, as difficult as it was, I knew in my heart I needed to proceed with succession planning—no more dodging the issue. I realized I needed to do what was best for ISI, not necessarily what was best for me.

I soon found that succession planning was not so much an event but more of a multi-year process. It simply takes time—a lot of time. And because succession planning and exit strategies do take so much time to develop, it is imperative for owners to start the discussion sooner rather than later. As an old Chinese proverb says, "The best time to plant a tree was twenty years ago; the second-best time is today." We settled for the second-best time and got to work.

Of course, initially we had more questions than answers, but after extensive research, we learned that developing a succession strategy included some fundamental steps:

1. Communicate the company's vision statement as well as future growth plans.
2. Get a clear picture of existing employee skill sets to match up with future career opportunities.
3. Ask employees about where they would like to be with their careers in two, five, and ten years
4. Carefully evaluate each employee's potential and determine where they may fit in the future organization.
5. Have a candid discussion with all employees (one-on-one if possible) to discuss their feelings about the succession plan and what it means to them.
6. Be honest and transparent in all communication with employees, and as much as possible, groom them according to

their individual skill sets, desired career path, and long-term potential.

Overall, a decision needed to be made about what the future of the business would look like once the exit strategy was in place. In our case, we had to ask ourselves even more difficult questions: Was ISI really building the business for the future? Was selling the company still an option? In 2015, with many valuations of technology companies coming in much lower than expected, selling ISI didn't really seem to be the best move. On the other hand, as I once heard Michael Gerber, author of *The E Myth: Why Most Small Businesses Don't Work and What to Do About It*, say, if you don't sell your business, that means you bought it. Assuming that as the owner of ISI I had decided to "buy" my business, then what?

I already knew we needed new leadership. So what should that leadership look like? In the turbulent world of technology, it made perfect sense to identify and nurture energetic young talent. As I thought about it, why not millennials (like my son, for instance) who could embrace change and move the business forward? Back in 2007, I implemented this very strategy when I replaced 80 percent of the company's sales team with millennials (the youngest working-age generation at the time). They may not have had any experience, but they helped us double ISI's business during the worst economy in eighty years, between 2007 and 2011. Hiring young people was one of the best moves I ever made and was well worth the risk and investment.

As the leadership team and I pondered the company's succession plan, we thought, why not use the same strategy to develop new leadership? Regardless of whether I intended to sell the business in the future or not, as an owner of a fast-paced technology firm, I needed to consistently bring on new personnel with new ideas. The more we thought about it, the more we realized there was a practical side to this issue as well. If I didn't plan to hire younger leadership, how else could I keep a business going for five, ten, or twenty more years?

After a number of meetings with trusted advisers and key employees and after gaining a keener understanding of succession planning, I developed the company's strategy for future growth, which, in essence, was the primary motivation for developing a succession plan. After experiencing several frustrating sales years in a row, I focused on growing the business and moving the needle, which was no easy task. I needed some new sales ideas to grow the business and generate positive energy to move the company forward.

I also had to admit that after years as CEO, I was getting increasingly weary of dealing with chronic issues around accounts receivable, problem employees, and accounts payable. Perhaps the one issue I was most tired of dealing with was the two-million-dollar line of credit with our bank. The question always hanging over my head was, *What if the company should falter?* My wife and I would be required to personally pay off the bank since that was the way ISI's line of credit was set up. For those reasons and several more, I didn't have the enthusiasm for the business I once had. It was clear it was time for a change.

Since ISI was a Myers family business, I wanted a family member to run it and continue the legacy. It meant a lot to me. My son Jordan became my obvious choice. However, nepotism wasn't the primary driver for my decision. Jordan had paid his dues at ISI, having worked for the company part time through high school and college, doing mostly grunt work in the company warehouse and in the customer service department. The work wasn't glamorous, but he was learning the business from the ground up. A few years later, Jordan subsequently opened the ISI Chicago office in 2015, which, in a short period of time, experienced significant sales success, landing several major accounts and establishing the company in a major metropolitan market. Jordan had built a good track record with ISI, so I felt he was more than qualified for the job as CEO.

So, we developed our succession plan. Jordan would move from Chicago to Memphis and work simultaneously as a member of the ISI sales team and also as CEO in training for the next three years. We both believed that would give him plenty of time to develop even stronger relationships with ISI employees, customers, and suppliers. He would then assume control of the company on January 1, 2019. On a side note, while we were going through all the stress and strain of the M&A process in 2018, Jordan personally sold over six million dollars in revenue, which accounted for more than 40 percent of ISI's total that year. Any questions or concerns about placing Jordan in the CEO role were answered emphatically.

And even though I was very clear about the decision to appoint Jordan as my successor, I did consider the feelings of long-term ISI employees who may have had an issue with my decision. After all, many on the ISI management team had paid their dues and may have felt more deserving of the role. Recognizing this could become a bigger issue in the future, we held one-on-one meetings with employees over the next year or so. In those meetings, I reviewed the succession plan and the logic behind it to get their buy in. I also assured employees and managers that I wasn't going anywhere and certainly wasn't planning to retire; rather, I was genuinely trying to position us for the future. As I told many in various meetings, it didn't make sense for a sixty-plus-year-old guy to run a tech company. Though painful to admit, the wise decision was to bring on a smart young leader who had the necessary energy and stamina to not only run the business but also keep up with all of the changes in technology.

Plus, as I looked around during the many calls I would make with the ISI sales team, I recognized that most of ISI's customers looked more like my son than me. It was undeniable that we had a younger customer base than ever before. Clearly, the world of technology had changed a lot since I started ISI in 1996, which was over two decades ago by then—more than a lifetime in technology. In my mind, it seemed like the perfect time for the transition.

So, in late 2016, Jordan and his wife relocated from Chicago to Memphis, and we immediately established him as ISI's future CEO. Over the next few years, Jordan shadowed me to learn the ropes firsthand. After all, he was only twenty-nine at the time and would be thirty-two when he took over the business. Many asked me, "Have you lost your mind?"

Was it hard to appoint my son as my successor? Of course it was. It was no secret that I loved owning a business and being positioned as "the man." For over two decades, it was all I knew. But for me, it still had to come down to what was best for my employees, customers, and business partners. I also reminded myself that it couldn't always be all about me; it was time to pass the torch.

ISI had finished 2016 with good but not great sales results. We had flatlined for the past four years and needed some kind of catalyst or jolt to move forward. Going into 2017, we hoped that catalyst would be my son, but he wouldn't take over for another two years. Both Jordan and I agreed it would take a lot of work to successfully execute the strategy. Succession planning can be a very arduous process and does not need to be rushed. It had to be done right since there was no margin for error and no opportunity for a do-over. It was my son's future and my legacy we were talking about.

In October 2016, Jordan joined the ISI sales team and was responsible for developing new business in Memphis and Mississippi. He brought in significant new business with a number of major healthcare accounts and focused his sales efforts on a new application, which involved integrating AV technology into medical simulation labs all across the country. And the best part? Most simulation projects represented big-time revenue and profit. This was exciting stuff with lots of growth potential. When Jordan wasn't selling, he was our CEO-in-training, learning the ins and outs of running the business and dealing with a wide range of issues, such as HR, accounts payable, accounts receivable, project management, and more. It didn't take long for Jordan to realize that being the CEO of ISI was not an easy job.

With the company-wide sales growth in 2017, every day presented a new challenge for our support employees and management. Jordan was getting a firsthand look at life in the hot seat as the company leader. It was both exciting and stressful, but since we were growing, it beat the alternative. Throughout 2017, the company maintained a level of profitability we hadn't seen in a number of years and was poised for even more growth in 2018.

So, for the record, how did we pull out of our sales slump? Truthfully, it was a combination of strategies, the first of which was to invest in areas that would better support our customers. Since over 90 percent of ISI's revenue came from repeat customers, this strategy was a no-brainer. We beefed up our customer service department to provide even higher quality support and added several new project managers to focus on key customers.

Second, we doubled down in sales and technical support for niche markets, such as distance learning, telemedicine, and corporate videoconferencing. That strategy in particular paid serious dividends in 2017 as we ended up having the second-best year in company history and the best year since 2011. ISI booked over twenty million in revenue in 2017 and grew the business 20 percent year over year, achieving record profitability. It was more than exciting. As we would find out a short time later, our performance that year got us noticed in the AV industry.

Meanwhile, I discovered that succession planning can be tricky business, particularly when dealing with family members. Early in

2018, Jordan approached me with the idea that we should formalize our succession planning agreement by drawing up legal documents. I have to admit, I was taken aback. This agreement had started out so simple and straightforward. Why did we have to go to all the expense of getting lawyers involved when it was an agreement between a father and his son? Each of us needed to have our own attorney? Really? At the time, I felt like I was in the middle of some kind of crazy legal battle and was not happy about it.

Jordan and I always had a great relationship, but I have to admit that I couldn't hide my disappointment in my son. My feelings were hurt, and I kept asking myself, *Why did he feel he had to lawyer up? Couldn't we draft our own agreement and save a lot of money?* To me, it made more sense than going through all of the legal mumbo jumbo that ends up making the lawyers a lot of money. More important, why didn't my son trust his own father? Many times during our legal discussions, I simply wanted to pull the plug and not go through with the succession plan at all. After all, it was my company (and life) we were talking about, and I didn't like the way this was going. I was shaking my head, trying to understand it all.

After several months and numerous additional discussions, Jordan and I ended up working through it all, creating a formal written document for transitioning the management of ISI to Jordan as of January 2019. We added a provision for him to "buy" equity in the business from me. In the agreement, we detailed how Jordan would accrue up to a 49 percent ownership stake in ISI over the next five years. From a financial perspective, it seemed a reasonable plan that would work out well for both Jordan and me.

In retrospect, and as much as I hate to admit it, putting all of it in writing was the right thing to do. Jordan now had a clear incentive to profitably grow the business for the next several years with an eye toward a potential liquidity event at some point in time. When it was all said and done, it made a lot of sense to both of us, and we were excited about the possibilities.

Though Jordan and I ended up with a succession plan we both felt good about, things in business (and life) don't always go as planned. As fate would have it, that potential liquidity event would come sooner than either of us expected.

Swing for the Fences

- Succession planning is not so much of an event as a multi-year process, so start sooner rather than later. It takes time to do it right.
- Succession planning can be tricky business, particularly when dealing with family members. Try to remember, it's just business, not personal, and legally document everything.
- Passing the torch is an emotional ride for any entrepreneur, so make sure you do it for the right reasons. Be honest with yourself.
- When appointing a successor, always focus on what's best for the business, not necessarily what's best for you personally.

Passing the torch to my son Jordan was highly emotional for me, but it was also the right thing to do.

Chapter 11

Confronting Myself: The Emotional Rollercoaster of Letting My Other Baby Go

In the process of letting go, you will lose many things from the past, but you will find yourself.

—Deepak Chopra

May 22, 2018

I was going through my normal morning routine of sorting through my messages when I picked up a voicemail from another one of those investment guys I had been dodging for years. I didn't intend to return the call, but somehow this message had a different sound to it. I figured it wouldn't cost me anything to at least hear him out.

When I returned the call, the conversation went something like this: "Mr. Myers, you may remember I talked to you over a year ago about potentially selling your company. Any chance you are interested in another conversation? The CEO of the largest AV integration firm in the world is interested in talking to you about a potential acquisition of ISI."

That got my attention. I was more than a little surprised. The largest AV integration firm in the world was interested in little ol' ISI? My reaction? Wow! As we continued the conversation, it was clear that the CEO of the potential acquirer really did want to have a discussion with me.

"How about meeting him in Las Vegas at InfoComm next month?" the investment guy asked.

InfoComm is the premier event in the AV industry and annually attracts over forty thousand customers, vendors, and integrators to its week-long technical/educational conference. It's the Super Bowl for most everybody in the AV business. But I had one small problem. I had no plans to attend InfoComm. I didn't have anything against Las Vegas, but since I wasn't going, I had planned to send several ISI employees to the conference. That included design engineers and a number of salespeople who viewed InfoComm as a reward for a job well done.

I tentatively answered, "I won't be attending InfoComm this year, but my son Jordan will be there. Maybe you can talk to him about the potential acquisition." In the back of my mind, I had confidence that Jordan could do a good job of vetting the company since he had done this for me back in 2014 with the other potential acquirer. I then added, "I've made a commitment to Jordan that he will be the next company CEO in 2019, so this discussion will be a short one unless it includes Jordan being placed in a high-level leadership role with the company." After all, it is what I had promised him when he moved back to Memphis from Chicago, and we both had gone through a lot of expensive legal work to make that happen. I also made it clear to the investment guy that I am a man of my word; when I make a commitment, I keep it. I thought this succession detail would be a deal killer, so at the end of the conversation, I was skeptical at best.

June 8, 2018

I was down in Florida when I got the call from Jordan. He had made it to Las Vegas and met with the potential acquirer. He liked what he heard.

"Dad, I think we may have something here. We have a lot in common with them." He sounded excited. "I really like their go-to-market strategy, particularly with pricing, margin expectations, and competitive positioning. And I have to tell you that we also share similar company values and culture. It could be a good fit."

Although I was surprised by my son's reaction, it sounded intriguing and was definitely worth a second look. So, we agreed to set up a video conference call in the next few weeks to discuss their interest further.

June 21, 2018

I'm not sure I knew what to expect when we finally connected on video with the CEO a few weeks later. After all, he was running the largest integration company in the AV industry with over eight hundred million in sales and more than two thousand employees, including forty-five offices in both the United States and abroad. In other words, they were big and impressive. When we got through our various introductions, it was time to get down to business.

I opened the meeting with a simple question for the CEO: "Why do I need you?" I then went on to explain, "ISI has competed with your company on major AV projects five times in the past few years, and we have beaten you all five times."

I wasn't trying to be a smart aleck, but I needed answers. Initially, the CEO seemed taken aback by my question, but then he gathered himself.

"That's the very point, Jay," he responded. "We've figured out that if we can't beat ISI, we need you to join us."

It was a clever response that resonated with both me and Jordan. We went on to talk about the advantages of being part of a larger organization, which included career opportunities for my employees as well as better benefits and the ability to relocate to satellites around the world. As the conversation continued, I realized those were things a smaller company like ISI simply couldn't provide. The CEO also pointed out the advantage of an acquisition for me and my wife. Once we sold the business, we no longer had to worry about day-to-day issues like the bank line of credit, aging accounts receivable, and human resource issues. It all sounded good, but I couldn't help but think that maybe it was too good to be true. Still, the discussion seemed worth pursuing, so we agreed to meet again in another week or so to see where that would take us.

June 28, 2018

On the next call we got into more detail about the potential acquirer's interest in ISI, which included pulling things like preliminary (audited) ISI financials, multi-state sales licenses, and a census of company employees. It seemed the intensity of the deal had definitely increased. At that point, we both agreed a confidentiality agreement or a non-disclosure agreement (NDA) needed to be signed by both companies to move to the next step. By signing the NDA, both parties could freely share information with each other and protect the integrity of the process.

On a totally different note, one thing I personally picked up on about the acquirer's mergers and acquisitions (M&A) team was how incredibly *polite* they were to Jordan and me. I was more than a little surprised at their demeanor. Why? Because almost everything I had ever heard about the M&A industry from friends and business associates was all negative. I was told by more than a few people that M&A was a really nasty business and that as time went on, many of the people involved in the acquisition could get incredibly ruthless and cruel, which almost always led to disastrous results. All too often the process left many an entrepreneur with a ton of regret about ever getting tangled up in the M&A world in the first place. Fortunately, Jordan and I seemed to be in a different position with our deal. We sincerely liked (and trusted) the firm interested in us. It was at that point we decided to continue to move forward with the process.

Things were getting more serious on both ends, which made me excited and nervous at the same time. Was this the time? Was I really going to let my baby go?

July 10, 2018

I quickly realized that the acquisition process is an extremely intense experience, and it seemed to get more intense every day. Every hour of every day we were required to submit even more information about ISI, including accounts payable and accounts receivable reports, tax records, company leases, and more. We had to retrieve a mountain of information in a short period of time, and I quickly realized I was not going to be the guy to do that. Did it make sense for the owner of the company to be snooping around for all of this sensitive information? Wouldn't that send up a red flag to my employees? Wouldn't they be concerned about what was going on? My thinking was that even the slightest hint of a potential acquisition would have freaked out our employees and possibly sunk the deal before it gained momentum. If word leaked out to our customers, it would be even scarier, so we decided to take a safer route. Jordan would be the point man on gathering the data, and if questioned, we would blame all of his requests on the succession-planning process. We figured everyone at ISI knew Jordan would soon be taking over as CEO anyway.

Every day for the next few weeks, Jordan secured additional pieces of information and put them into a data room for both companies to review. And while all of this was going on, we still had a company to run. How much more information would they need? There seemed to be no end in sight, and we still had no idea what kind of offer they had in mind. I was trying desperately not to take my eye off the ball, but that was easier said than done. Where was this all going? Were we wasting our time with these guys? On the other hand, when we did get our answer, it would be decision time. Did I really want to sell ISI? I'd been in my role for so long that my employees felt more like my children than just company workers. How do you sell your children? It was a gut-wrenching time, but I knew I needed to see this opportunity through or possibly regret it for the rest of my life.

July 24, 2018

We reached the point in the process where many accounting and legal questions had to be answered, and it was evident I was getting in way over my head. If I wanted to make sure I didn't make a costly misstep, I would need to get some additional professional support.

That's when I reached out to ISI's long-term accounting firm as well our corporate attorney. Both had extensive M&A experience and were people I could trust implicitly. In fact, the owner of the accounting firm and I had gone to college together back in the 1970s, so our friendship spanned several decades. Beyond that, he and his firm had done a great job supporting ISI for over fifteen years.

Also, our corporate attorney had a special place in my heart. Our relationship went back to the late 1990s when she helped me buy out my partner in a nasty business divorce. Since ISI was not making any money then, it was a particularly critical time for both me and the company. If it hadn't been handled just right, ISI could have been finished before it ever got started. But our attorney got the job done, and the rest, as they say, is history.

Armed with a strong legal and accounting team, Jordan and I got to work handling the various requests that the acquirer continued to make on a daily basis. I then realized that the M&A process was definitely not for the faint of heart. It was evident we would need strong accounting and legal support to bring the acquisition to a successful conclusion. I thought, *Why would I not want to leverage all my available resources to help with the biggest deal of my career?* I also reminded myself that this was not a time to cut corners or attempt to do it myself. The stakes were just too high.

I must reiterate how important it is for a company to have strong ongoing accounting and legal support to protect you, your family, and your business. And this applies to all small business owners whether you choose to sell your business in the future or not.

Yet after all this frenzy of activity, we still didn't have an offer. And that made me more than a little nervous.

July 31, 2018

The intensity of the deal moved to yet another level as we focused on the sales and profit numbers as well as ISI's overall financial position. I noticed how impressed the M&A representative was with the fact that ISI was debt free and had zeroed out our line of credit. They even noted that ISI had one of the cleanest balance sheets they had ever seen, which we were glad to hear. They also noted there were no unusual charges by the owner at ISI, like charging the company for a lake house, paying for a boat or motorcycle, or covering some other elaborate personal expense, which they had seen in the financials of other private companies. None of that was going on at ISI, and it made an impression on the M&A representative. He saw we were trustworthy and squeaky clean.

As time went on, we shared information on profit margins, project backlog, sales forecasts, and projected overhead expenses (payroll, rent, leases, etc.). In addition, there was a specific interest in ISI's service contracts, which were coincidentally the most profitable product/service we had. As we continued to provide more and more financial information, it became very evident why these guys were interested in ISI. We were profitable and had been for over twenty years. We also had spent the time and money to generate audited financials every year, which many small companies simply don't bother with because of the cost. Having audited financials readily available was also very helpful in speeding up the M&A process.

That's when we learned perhaps the most important lesson of all. You want a company to have interest in acquiring your firm? It's not that complicated. *Make money* every year and have the audited financials to back you up. Many of my fellow entrepreneurs and small business owners still don't get this basic concept. Many of them are smart but have a false impression of what their businesses is really worth. I will reiterate that it is not what you *think* your business is worth but what somebody is willing to pay for it that matters.

Another lesson I learned (as noted in previous chapters) was that acquirers had a lot of interest in buying companies with some sort of recurring revenue, like service contracts and repeat customers. In our case, we were doing two million dollars' worth of service contracts annually, and 90 percent of our company revenue was generated from repeat customers. That translates into *value*, and it was a strong calling card for ISI. In the end, we came to realize that the most important number is not the total revenue but the overall bottom-line profit.

We also learned that in the M&A process, timing is everything. For us, it didn't hurt that ISI had just experienced its second-best revenue/profit year in 2017, which we suspected was why we were targeted for acquisition six months later. As fate would have it, we were informed that an offer would be made in our next video meeting. It was getting real, but as I would soon find out, the rollercoaster ride was just beginning.

August 6, 2018

As you can imagine, Jordan and I greatly anticipated the upcoming video call. So much work had already been done to get to this point, but so many questions were still buzzing around in my head: *What kind of number would they come up with? Would it be worth our while to continue the M&A process? Would this be life-changing money for me and my family? How would I handle somebody else running the company that I created? How would my employees and customers respond?*

I also couldn't ignore that for over twenty-two years I had loved being an entrepreneur. ISI was my pride and joy, just like my children were. Owning my own successful business had been the high point of my career to that point. What would come next?

When we finally connected over video, I was a nervous wreck. As we all sat down, it didn't take long to get the answer we were looking for. A few minutes into the call, the M&A team made the offer. Jordan and I just looked at each other and didn't give them an immediate response. The initial offer seemed to be in the ballpark I had been thinking of, but there was a lot to consider. Like any good businessman, I also knew that the first offer wasn't the last one, so I countered with a higher number. They responded that they would have to get back to us in a few days. I also said I would need to talk it over with my wife before I could make a final decision.

At that point, I had to pinch myself. *Is this really happening? Will twenty-two years of hard work finally pay off? Will they come back with the right number?* Those were just a few of the questions buzzing in my head for yet another sleepless night.

August 8, 2018

We connected on video early that morning and got our answer on the counteroffer. Although it wasn't exactly the number we wanted, we did feel the offer was fair and decided to move forward. Once the offer was accepted, that's when the *real* work began. In the M&A world, this is known as *due diligence*. Not only was this the most arduous part of the whole process, but it also tested me both physically and mentally.

On top of that, the M&A representative sent us the letter of intent (LOI) to sign. As we discovered, the LOI was needed to formalize their offer in writing. As part of the process, both parties agreed to meet in person so we could get to know each other better. That meant that the whole M&A team and corporate executives (including the private equity representative) would fly into Memphis to meet with us. The agenda included a number of discussion items, such as marketing, sales, corporate finance, and operating strategies. On top of that, the M&A team wanted to see the ISI office and visit some of our key customers. It would be a very full day. It was getting harder and harder to run a company as I was trying to sell it, but that's exactly what I had to do. The emotional summer continued.

August 29, 2018

We finally met face-to-face with the M&A manager and the corporate executive team, which included the COO, SVP of Sales, CEO, and private equity representative. For confidentiality purposes, we agreed to meet at the ISI accounting firm's office, which not only worked logistically for all of us but would also be a convenient location should there be additional accounting or finance questions. It was an intense experience, with each executive asking a boatload of questions on a variety of issues. We held our own, though. They wanted to know *everything* about me and ISI and left no stone unturned. It was also interesting how much they wanted to know about ISI's corporate clients and repeat business, as well as our customer service department and the company's intellectual property. They seemed particularly impressed with ISI-Net, our remote management tool for our healthcare clients.

They repeated many times that "we have paid attention to Tennessee," and that they were keenly interested in getting a foothold in the state. It made me think of the saying, "People buy for their reasons, not yours." In our case, their reasons to acquire ISI seemed to have as much to do with geography as anything else. And that wasn't a bad thing.

At that point in the meeting, I started to come to terms with the magnitude of what we were doing. My mind wandered back to 1996, when I started the company, and all the obstacles we had overcome to get to this point. Truthfully, that moment was a surreal experience, one I had dreamed about for over twenty years but never really thought would happen. Yet here I was, seeing it all unfold in front of my eyes.

Later that same day, we visited several of ISI's major accounts, which, of course, we did under the cloak of secrecy. I have to admit it felt more than a little weird since I am not a deceptive person by nature. I have always prided myself on running ISI with complete transparency, so arranging these secret visits almost felt like betrayal. But as I soon discovered, it was all part of the typical M&A process.

After visiting the ISI office (after hours, of course), Jordan and I then went out to dinner with the CEO, where we were joined by both my wife and daughter-in-law. I loved the CEO's remark as we were sitting down for dinner: "Since we want to buy a family business, we would love to meet the rest of the family." That remark impressed me and helped increase my comfort level with the whole deal—and so did the way the CEO interacted with my wife and daughter-in-law. He was so down-to-earth and sincere that I couldn't help but like the guy.

After dinner, when I was dropping the CEO off at his hotel, we got into a brief discussion about the emotions I was feeling about selling my baby. I told him how much I was beating myself up mentally, that I wasn't sure selling ISI was the right thing to do.

To this day I will never forget his response. He said, "Jay, I understand what it's like to be in a startup. As CFO, I observed firsthand the founder's personal attachment to the business. I get it." Then he added, "It's not lost on me that you have entrusted me with your legacy." I couldn't believe what I just heard. All I could think was *Wow!* On my drive back home that night, I realized that these people really did get it. At that point I had more clarity than ever about the whole M&A process and why I was selling ISI. I knew at that moment I was selling to the right people.

September 12, 2018

The thirty days after the offer was accepted went by in a blur, and I realized the process was taking a toll on me personally and professionally. Even though we had a solid offer, and despite the clarity I experienced that night after dinner with the CEO, I continued to second guess myself. My own words were coming back to haunt me. More than a few times I had told my team, "I didn't start ISI to make a bunch of money, and I won't end it for a bunch of money." *Am I being hypocritical?* I kept asking myself.

On top of that, selling ISI was just one of the topics my wife and I discussed on a daily basis that summer. There was also that little matter of planning our daughter's wedding, which was a little more than a month away—no small task. Because it was a destination wedding (Savannah) and we had to remotely manage everything from Memphis, it was more than a little maddening.

Between the acquisition and the wedding, things were getting so intense around the house that my wife made sure to have my cardiologist's cell phone number on speed dial. She was that concerned. Fortunately, as time went on, she never had to make that call. But it was also at that point when both my wife and I had to acknowledge that, with all the life-changing events going on, we were feeling overwhelmed, which was not a good thing. So, as time went on, we both committed to keeping it together and not letting all the craziness get to us.

Even though the offer, the NDA, and the LOI were all signed by both parties, I was still in conflict. *Was I doing the right thing? What if I declined the offer? What would life look like for me post-ISI? Why did I feel like I was leading a double life?* Add in wedding planning, and life at home was getting more stressful by the minute.

It wasn't any better at the ISI office, with all the video calls and even more conference calls between the M&A representative, me, Jordan, our attorney, and our accountant. Most calls were made during normal business hours, but still more were late in the evening (including midnight) and weekends. The private equity rep was determined to close the sale in October, preferably earlier in the month rather than later.

That may have been what *they* wanted, but there was another major event going on in October that I would be a part of, whether the sale of ISI went through or not. For some time, my daughter's wedding had been scheduled for October 27. I remember repeatedly telling the M&A team that this was my one and only daughter, who was also my baby, and I would not let them or anybody else distract me on my daughter's big day.

To their credit, they understood, and the target closing date was set on October 31, 2018—exactly *four days* after my daughter's wedding. Talk about life in the fast lane.

Meanwhile, I was getting a crash course on terms important to the deal that everyone involved in the sale seem to be familiar with except me. One important term that came up time and time again was *net working capital calculation*, which is the difference between a company's current assets (such as cash, accounts receivable, and inventory) and its current liabilities (such as accounts payable). In essence, it is a measure of a company's liquidity and a key element in establishing the terms of the sale.

Another term I had to get familiar with was *peg,* or *true-up,* which I soon found out is an important part of the M&A process where millions of dollars can be at stake. Yet many small business owners know very little about it, including me until this process began. A peg represents a fixed-dollar amount based on historical levels of working capital (identified in audited financials) in the business. And it can have significant implications. In fact, the net working capital calculation became a very important issue when the time came for ISI to close on the sale because there was a lot of money at stake. The way it works is that whenever the level of the ISI net working capital exceeded the established target, then ISI was owed the difference in a cash payment.

Conversely, should the level of ISI net working capital not meet the established target, then the acquirer would make an adjustment to the purchase price prior to closing. In most cases, since company sales, work in process, accounts payable, and accounts receivable can literally vary on a daily basis, there is almost always a payment of some nature (to either the buyer or seller) that is reflected in an adjustment typically made before or at closing. Ultimately the whole point of calculating a working capital peg for ISI was to determine the appropriate level of working capital that the company needed to run the business day-to-day, no more and no less. I have to admit it became the *key* topic of discussion between me, our attorney, and our accountant every other day for several weeks. It was exhausting, but it was important because a lot of money was at stake. And because so much money was at stake, I was quite happy I had put together a great legal and accounting support team to protect me and ensure no money would be left on the table.

I was also once again reminded that selling a business is a very big deal with very little room for error. The crazy thing is, even with all the effort put forth up to this point by both parties, M&A statistics show that a large percentage of acquisitions fall apart (for a wide variety of reasons) before closing. It got me thinking: *Will ISI be among the small percent who have a successful closing? Will there be any last-minute surprises?* We were about to find out.

September 26, 2018

I had several more weeks of conference calls with our accountant and our corporate attorney to discuss a wide variety of issues related to ISI's customer base, multi-state tax filings, and revenue streams. I have to say that the company interested in buying us was incredibly thorough, and retrieving all the information they needed continued to weigh on me. I felt a lot of pressure to get this deal done before the end of October. Every day it became more difficult to keep it all from my employees, business partners, customers, and suppliers. But we plowed ahead and felt we could see the light at the end of the tunnel.

Then I got a call from our accounting firm who made a recommendation about the proceeds from the sale. Specifically, they wanted to look into whether some of the money could be paid to me as "personal goodwill" to save me a lot of money in taxes. Apparently, the tax rate for personal goodwill was as much as 16 percent lower than the standard corporate tax rate, which had the potential for significant savings for me after closing.

How does an owner calculate his or her value to the business so that it would be considered "personal goodwill"? I had no idea. I was told it was a simple matter of having a third party conduct a valuation to determine how much of ISI's business was a direct result of my personal involvement. So I contacted a local Memphis-based company that specialized in this type of valuation and proceeded to meet with them for many, many hours discussing the various contracts, key clients, earned revenue, and profit I had personally had a hand in over the past twenty years. It was yet another exhausting process, but it was worth it.

It became very obvious to me that personal goodwill is not an arbitrary number owners can just give acquirers in hopes it will save them money. It had to be documented by a qualified auditing firm, which is exactly what was done.

After the audit was completed and submitted to the M&A team, they appeared satisfied with the results of the valuation and agreed to move forward. I immediately called our accountant and expressed my gratitude to his team for making such a good recommendation. Though I had made it a habit to challenge the bills from our accounting firm in the past, in this case they were worth more than their weight in gold. I was more than willing to pay them for providing me important advice at such a crucial time for both me and ISI.

As I looked at the calendar, I realized we were just a little over forty-five days from closing the biggest deal of my career. The questions began again: *What else do I need to do before the closing? Have I missed anything—will there be any surprises? Am I doing the right thing?*

October 26, 2018

Weeks went by in a blur in Memphis. So much information passed hands between so many people, with an endless number of conference calls and emails. But now I was in a hotel room in Savannah, very excited to be getting ready for my daughter's wedding the next day. I was especially looking forward to seeing the cathedral and being a part of the rehearsal dinner that night.

I was finally ready to put everything aside regarding the sale of the business and focus on my family—more specifically, my daughter. As a promise to my wife, I had even left my computer at home so I wouldn't have any work-related distractions. As fate would have it, I had been at the hotel for a short period of time when I received an urgent email from the M&A team requesting my signature (and my wife's) on some closing documents. *How am I supposed to do that when I am in a hotel room in Savannah and my computer is back in Memphis?* I asked myself.

I grabbed Jordan and headed to the hotel business center to fire up one of their computers. As we were responding to the email, we got another surprise when my soon-to-be son-in-law dropped in to see what was going on and kill time before the rehearsal dinner. After making up a story about how we were trying to retrieve an important purchase order for ISI, we finished copying the requested information on a flash drive and headed out the door. It was so cloak and dagger, I remarked to Jordan that I felt like we were behaving like some kind of secret agents. *Why in the hell couldn't they have gotten this information from us two weeks ago?* I thought in frustration.

I would soon find out, after speaking to several of my business associates (after the fact), that these last-minute requests are a standard part of the M&A process, which tends to be fast, furious, and unpredictable before closing. Even in Savannah, getting ready for my daughter's wedding, I was still on the M&A rollercoaster. Thankfully, our closing date was only five days away, and I was hoping and praying that the stress and tension of the past six months would be worth all the trouble.

October 31, 2018

The acquiring company's executive team and M&A representative all gathered in the ISI conference room with me, my son, and all of ISI's employees. The big day had finally arrived, and my son and I were decked out in business suits and ties in honor of the occasion. Everyone else, including the acquiring company's executive team, was dressed casual with corporate logos on their shirts. It made for an interesting contrast.

As I walked into the ISI conference room, it felt a little more than surreal. As I looked around the room at all my employees, my eyes wandered to the seven *Inc.* 5000 plaques on the walls we had earned for being one of the fastest growing private companies in the country. It was such an incredible accomplishment, and I was proud of our staff. Then my mind went back to the early days of ISI, our fight for survival, and all that we had been through together, from a cancer diagnosis, a painful business divorce, an embezzlement, and losing and rebuilding 80 percent of our sales team during the Great Recession. I was so proud of my young team when they doubled business amidst the worst economy in eighty years.

After signing a few more documents, it was time to let my other baby go. In my mind, I knew this was going to be an emotional day for me, and it was shaping up to be that and much more. When it came time for me to speak, I informed the ISI employees about the sale and explained it was primarily done for the overall betterment of the company and their careers. I also pointed out the many advancement and relocation opportunities they would soon have with the new company. They would also have access to better healthcare and other benefits with an eight-hundred-million-dollar company supporting them. The big plus (for me) that I pointed out was that with strong financial support, ISI had an opportunity to grow to its full potential over the next few years.

I thought I had made some good points, but I could easily see the look of disappointment on their faces. After a minute or so of stunned silence, I then opened it up for questions. The very first question was from our Nashville design engineer.

"You just married your daughter off four days ago, and now you're letting your business go? Dude, I'm surprised you're not in the hospital!"

"Maybe I should be," I chuckled.

He was right. Letting go of my daughter and my business within one week was absolute insanity. The amount of stress my family and I had endured over the past six months was hard to comprehend. At the time, I was thinking it was a miracle we were able get through all of it and keep it together. But in my heart, I knew that my daughter had married the right guy and I had sold my business to the right company. I was at peace. After answering a few more employee questions, the meeting wrapped up.

Then I realized that this was it, the end of an era for me, my family, and ISI. My experience as an entrepreneur had been a rollercoaster ride since day one and challenged me in so many ways. Yet, as I looked back, I believed my time with ISI gave me the ability to develop the best version of myself, both personally and professionally, and to live out my dream. For that I would always be grateful.

My mind then wandered to a recent conversation I had with one of my friends who had asked me, "If you had known about all the crazy obstacles and challenges that were going to happen to you and ISI over the past twenty years, would you still have started the company?"

I thought for a minute and then responded, "Absolutely."

When it was time for me to leave and walk out of the room, I did so with tears in my eyes and a lump in my throat. I stopped for a minute and thought to myself, *It's been one helluva ride.*

Swing for the Fences

- Be sure to assemble a solid professional team to support you during the acquisition process, including a lawyer and an accountant with M&A experience. Don't even think about going it alone. In fact, outside of the M&A process, a small business owner needs to have strong, on-going legal and accounting support for the lifetime of the business.
- You may think your work is done when you accept the offer, but it's actually just beginning. The due diligence stage is by far the most difficult part of the M&A process and will require a significant amount of your attention on a daily basis.

- Identify a trusted employee who can secure needed documents, reports, and licenses each day during the due diligence stage. As the business owner, you don't want to send up red flags by trying to do it yourself.

- Make sure the trusted employee understands the importance of confidentiality as any hint of selling your business could have a negative effect on employees, customers, and suppliers.

- Trying to sell your business while you are still running it is a nerve-wracking experience, so do whatever you can to stay focused on your day-to-day responsibilities as the owner. Let your professional team (accountant and lawyer) earn their pay by helping with the rest of the M&A process.

The day that the Interactive Solutions (ISI) sign was taken off the building was gut-wrenching for me, but I knew in my heart that it was time to let my other baby go.

Chapter 12

Don't Cry Because It's Over; Smile Because It Happened

It's always bittersweet to sell your business. But hopefully you're never really selling the business; you're investing in its future.
—Jimmy Dunne

S elling a small business you've built over many years, or even decades, is never easy. But for many entrepreneurs, like me, the hardest part isn't preparing the business for the marketplace or finding the right time to exit. The hardest part is that I invested a significant portion of my life in my business. Over time, I had built a personal connection to the company, and for better or worse, ISI had become an important part of my family's daily life.

ISI had always been so much more than a business to me. It was my life's work, my professional identity, and the high point of my career. When it was time to say goodbye, I really did feel like I was losing a member of my family. It was heartbreaking. I was dealing with such a wide range of emotions: sorrow, anger, and fear, as well as a tremendous sense of loss. *What had I just done? Had I just made a huge mistake? What would my future look like without ISI?*

During the weeks and months after the sale, I received many emails, texts, and personal notes from friends and business associates congratulating me on the sale and wishing me the best of luck in the next chapter of my life. It was all so rewarding, and I was humbled by the outpouring of support. But it was also scary to close out one chapter of my life and start a whole new one. I kept thinking I should be happy about the sale and recognize that I had just achieved something many other entrepreneurs could only dream of.

But as those weeks and months went by, I kept having a nagging feeling that simply wouldn't go away. It was like I was still in conflict about the acquisition and continued to question my decision to sell. I kept asking myself, *Why don't I feel better about selling my business? Why do I have such an empty feeling about the whole experience?*

As a salesman, I naturally got caught up in making the sale. For several months, it was like going through a hurricane, and only now did I have the chance to think about what I had just sold.

Truthfully, I also felt some guilt about "selling out." I knew many of my employees weren't happy about my decision. Who could blame them? They had joined a family business and had been loyal to both me and ISI. Now that was all about to change. It would take time for them (and me) to adjust. I realized that selling the small business I had built over many years was never an easy proposition. It wasn't just a financial transaction; it was a life-changing moment for both me and my family, and it would take time to process and move forward.

As time marched on, I continued to deal with the emotional fallout from the sale. The day the ISI sign was removed on our building and replaced with the new company's logo, I was heartbroken. Even though

I had done what I thought was best for me and my family, it still felt bittersweet. Deep down I had to trust that I had done everything I could for ISI and that the company would grow even more without me. I also prayed I had left a positive legacy of leadership behind.

Several months after the sale, I was visiting my daughter in Atlanta. She asked me to stop by the department store where she worked because she wanted to give me my Christmas present in person. When I was handed the beautifully wrapped gift bag, I had a feeling something special was in it. I was right. Inside the bag was a framed picture of our first dance at the wedding. Surrounding the picture were the words to the song "Golden Lady" by Stevie Wonder. I was blown away. All the personal and professional emotions of the past few months finally caught up with me. I struggled to fight back the tears, but at that point, it just wasn't possible. I hugged my daughter and proceeded to cry like a baby.

Once you've reached the mountaintop, where do you go from there? Over the years I've observed many of my fellow entrepreneurs scratching and clawing to build their businesses without ever considering an exit strategy. They simply don't think about or talk about how to gracefully leave their business if they ever had to or wanted to; they don't envision what they would do next. For many, the topic is too difficult and too emotional to deal with, so they take the easy way out and ignore it. I get it; even thinking about leaving a business you started is difficult. You spend so many years building relationships with your employees, suppliers, customers, and colleagues that over time they can start feeling like family, which makes it even harder to let go.

But as I mentioned earlier, I realized it just didn't make sense to keep dodging an issue that had massive consequences for me, my family, and my company. Not having an exit strategy puts your family and business at greater risk should something happen to you. Also, by continuing to have this work-until-I-die mentality, owners make themselves particularly vulnerable to unanticipated events (economic downturn, recession, etc.) that can harm or destroy their businesses as well as their families. And in my case, did I really want to continue to put my family's personal savings at risk by constantly signing off on a line of credit year after year? And at the end of the day, did I want to be selling technology when I turned seventy?

That is why I decided to start working on my exit strategy (and my life after ISI) more than ten years before the sale. Building an exit strategy is simply not something you wake up one day and decide to do. It takes time to do it right. Even though I had no idea when or if a liquidity event might occur, I knew I needed to have a plan in place if it did happen.

For example, community service has always been important to me. It was also the way I was raised. As a business owner, I viewed community service as an obligation, not an option. After further self-examination I came to realize that I have always wanted to make a difference in my local community, specifically by leveraging my experience as an entrepreneur to help others chase the American dream of starting their own business. So, years ago, I started reaching out to the local entrepreneurial community in Memphis. The way I saw it, I felt very fortunate for the success of ISI and wanted to give back any way I could.

After the sale of my business, I simply expanded the work I had been doing all along: helping local budding entrepreneurs get their businesses off the ground and reach the next level. For the past several years, I have been mentoring young entrepreneurs at places like the University of Memphis and Christian Brothers University. I have met so many bright students through the years who are so excited about starting their own business. Their energy and enthusiasm is contagious. I feel younger just being around them.

In addition to giving back to colleges and universities, as I mentioned earlier, I have had the opportunity to work with and present to other small business owners and entrepreneurs at places like Start Co., a Memphis-based business incubator/accelerator. Start Co.'s Summer of Acceleration program, which prepares company founders to reach the next level in their business, has attracted entrepreneurs and business owners from all around the country. Interestingly enough, many of the Start Co. companies are built on digital platforms and are developing innovative apps for healthcare, trucking, and logistics, which I have found absolutely fascinating.

Besides helping entrepreneurs in the local area, for many years, I have also connected with universities such as the University of Tampa, Emory University, Belmont University, State College of Florida (SCF), DePaul University, Oklahoma State, and Duke University, where I have lectured on entrepreneurship and offered business advice to students who are not only fun to be around but always eager to learn. I've also had the pleasure to be involved with the Collegiate Entrepreneurs Organization (CEO), an entrepreneurship network with chapters on university campuses across North America and beyond.

I am flattered to have been a regular breakout speaker at the CEO National Conference, which annually attracts over one thousand attendees from all across the country. CEO is a dynamic organization, and I hope to support them for many years to come.

As I talk with these young entrepreneurs, I often share my own story of dealing with obstacles and overcoming adversity, in hopes of providing a source of encouragement. In 2007, to share my story with a wider audience, I wrote *Keep Swinging* and then followed it up six years later with *Hitting the Curveballs*. Writing these books was a cathartic experience for me, but I didn't realize at the time I was also paving the way toward a second career. Once the books were published, I received invitations to speak, not only at colleges and universities but at a number of high-profile business events as well. It was exciting. Those experiences got me thinking about my future and the role my books might play in my life after ISI. And that was thirteen years ago.

Truthfully, my goal in writing my books has always been to help readers by sharing the ups and downs of starting and growing a business from someone who has been there and done that. I also wanted entrepreneurs to learn from the many mistakes I made with ISI and avoid some of the pitfalls we experienced through the years. At each presentation, I regularly provide each student and/or business owner with a copy of one of my books (*Keep Swinging, Hitting the Curveballs*, or now, *Rounding Third and Heading for Home*). All these years later, I continue to be so gratified by all the emails, phone calls, and personal notes I receive from entrepreneurs all across the country. These same entrepreneurs have told me how my books struck a chord with them and provided much-needed inspiration in dealing with obstacles and adversity, not only in their businesses but in their personal lives as well.

For the past fourteen years, I've also supported Memphis entrepreneurs and small business owners through local groups like the Society of Entrepreneurs (SOE). As a member of the society, I have been actively involved with monthly SOE Roundtables and Insights Group, where members of the society have the opportunity to offer business advice and counsel to dozens of local small business owners on a regular basis. Being a part of SOE reminds me how much I love helping other people, and it has been an honor and a privilege to be part of SOE Memphis. In the second half of my career, I am looking forward to continuing to offer my assistance to this fine organization.

In addition to my work with the entrepreneurial community, I also serve on the executive committee and board of the Better Business Bureau of the Mid-South (www.bbb.org). The BBB is doing great work by promoting marketplace integrity and ethics in the local community, and I strongly believe in their mission. Not only have I enjoyed serving on the BBB board, but I have also personally benefited from many valuable relationships with prominent business owners and community leaders who serve on the BBB board. As I tell my kids all the time, "You are who you associate with." In my case, I am proud to say my associates are the best of the best.

I also continue to give back to my alma mater, the University of Memphis, where I am currently the executive in residence at the Fogelman College of Business and Economics (FCBE) teaching a public speaking class (Persuasive Presenter) as part of the Complete Professional Program (CPP). Although it is a non-paying position (I do have an office and a parking pass!), I have thoroughly enjoyed every minute of it. As part of my role as executive in residence, I've been asked to speak at university events like the FCBE Honors Banquet, as well as numerous executive and international MBA classes, which is always very flattering. On a personal note, I do think it's hilarious that the U of M has asked me to speak to these particular groups since I wasn't anywhere near an honors student back in the day, nor did I even try to pursue an MBA. But as I always tell the students, I did work my way through school, and I am proud of all of those Cs and my 2.34 GPA.

At this point in my career, these are just some of the organizations and groups that have touched my heart and continue to bring me the most joy. Working with them has been a true labor of love. Other organizations my wife and I are proud to support include the Church Health Center in Memphis, which is the largest faith-based, privately funded healthcare organization in the United States. Church Health is the medical home to tens of thousands of uninsured and underserved individuals and families across Shelby County, Tennessee. In fiscal year 2019 alone, Church Health saw more than 18,500 patients and had more than 62,500 patient encounters. The work of my friend and fellow SOE member Dr. Scott Morris and the Church Health team has made a life-saving difference to their patients in Memphis.

I am also proud to continue to support my high school alma mater, Christian Brothers High School, where I have been asked to speak to entrepreneurship and New Ventures classes for the past several years. I've been impressed with these high school students who have an interest in starting their own business. Back in the day, an entrepreneur was typically thought to be someone who started their own company because they couldn't get a regular job. These days, not only is owning your own business considered a respected profession but every entrepreneur I encounter is convinced they will be the next Bill Gates or Mark Zuckerberg and build billion-dollar empires as well. I appreciate their enthusiasm and lofty goals as there's nothing wrong with aiming high. Also, as a veteran business owner, I have to admit it's fun to see how times have changed and how interest in entrepreneurship has grown so dramatically.

Looking back, I will always be proud of my twenty-three years at ISI and appreciate the impact the company has had on my career and my life. I have to admit, I still have my bittersweet moments when I question my decision to sell the business. But as many of my friends and business associates have reminded me, having that feeling is totally understandable. And these days I am working hard on the future, not the past, and am focused on not just being successful but also significant. In the coming years, I want to create a legacy my family and I can all be proud of and leave a positive mark on our community. Thanks to spending the previous decade nurturing broader interests and developing my exit strategy for the long term, I am now very excited about these opportunities to reinvent myself and give back to my community.

Finally, I also feel fortunate to live in a country where a goofball like me has the opportunity to start and grow a successful business and live out his dream. When I look back on all the ups and downs of being a business owner, I remind myself of the quote a wise friend recently shared with me: "Don't cry because it's over. Smile because it happened."

Swing for the Fences

- Selling a business you spent many years building will never be easy, so be prepared for the emotional ride of your life.
- Selling your business is so much more than a financial transaction and will be a life-changing moment, not just for you but for your family as well.
- Develop an exit strategy well before you begin the process of selling your business. Doing so makes the post-sale transition a whole lot smoother for you and your family.
- Selling your business can feel like losing a member of your family and can be heartbreaking if you focus on the loss. Instead, view selling your business as investing in its future.

Giving my acceptance speech at the Society of Entrepreneurs induction ceremony. It is an honor and privilege to be part of this wonderful organization.

Speaking to entrepreneurship students at Belmont University in Nashville. Love their energy and enthusiasm!

It was such an honor to speak to students at the University of South Florida (USF) about exit strategies and life after selling my business.

I have spoken to college students all across the country, but the day I spoke to students at Duke University was particularly special.

Afterword

Over the past twenty-three years, I thought I had dealt with just about every possible crisis a small business owner could go through.

But nothing I have been through personally or professionally even remotely compares to the challenges we all face in 2020. As I write this book, people around the world are dealing with a healthcare crisis like nothing we have ever seen before: the 2019–20 coronavirus pandemic.

The outbreak was identified in Wuhan, China, in December 2019, and was recognized as a pandemic by the World Health Organization on March 11, 2020. As of early July 2020, COVID-19 has taken the lives of hundreds of thousands of Americans. And it's also had a dramatic impact on the US economy, delivering a potentially lethal blow to hundreds of thousands of restaurants, stores, and other small businesses across the country. Those same businesses find themselves suddenly isolated from their customers as so many Americans seek refuge from the lethal pandemic.

The US economy lost millions of jobs from March to July 2020. As of June 2020, nearly 33 million people were collecting unemployment, five times that of the Great Recession and more than any other time in modern history.[5] Small businesses have been hit especially hard by the crisis as they often have fewer resources and limited capital to draw on during an economic slowdown.

The economic reality of the pandemic has been different for each small business. As of May 2020, just over half of small businesses were closed temporarily, with many expecting to close permanently.[6] An incredibly heartbreaking situation.

The financial toll directly affects thousands of small business owners who have personally invested many years of blood, sweat, and tears in a company now in jeopardy of failure. And it's not their fault. But as challenging as it is in the world today, business worries seem particularly irrelevant when family members, friends, and others are diagnosed with a COVID-19 infection and must fight for their lives.

Given all that is going on, it is certainly more than understandable for entrepreneurs and small business owners to be incredibly anxious these days. These are trying times, the likes of which we have never seen before. But maintaining a high level of anxiety is certainly not healthy and definitely not part of an entrepreneur's mindset. Entrepreneurs by nature are perpetual optimists who always maintain a can-do attitude no matter the circumstances. When you stop and think about it, as entrepreneurs, if we weren't optimistic by nature, many small businesses would never have been created in the first place.

Communities across the United States have taken swift and drastic action to slow the spread of COVID-19. Many private and public schools have closed, countless major events have been canceled, and professional sports have come to a screeching halt (or restarted with no fans), so businesses large and small have been forced to change their day-to-day operations to merely survive. Colleges and universities across the country have made the decision to move their curriculum online and teach via distance learning. I myself am currently using Zoom videoconferencing software to remotely connect with and teach my University of Memphis FCBE students from my home in Florida.

In times like these, many struggle to know exactly what to do from one day to the next. And there are no easy answers. That's especially true for entrepreneurs and small business owners, who not only have to manage their businesses in this incredibly difficult environment but also have the obligation to take care of their employees, family members, and communities. How do people deal with so much fear and uncertainty amid the COVID-19 pandemic? What are some coping strategies? How do you survive day-to-day? How do you manage fear? Many questions with few answers.

I recently listened to a podcast by the author Simon Sinek who was commenting about the COVID-19 crises and its effect on the business world. He noted that *everything* is going to change as a result of the pandemic and that businesses would have to reinvent themselves to merely survive. He suggested that instead of asking questions like, "How do we do what we've been doing?" we need to ask, "How do we do what we've been doing in a different world?" And instead of asking, "How are we going to get through this?" we need to ask, "How are we going to change to get through this?"

While I certainly don't pretend to have the answers to these complex questions, I do believe in this country and our ability to persevere in the most difficult times. It is who we are. Through the years we have proven time and time again that in the moments of crisis we "answer the bell."

Also, as entrepreneurs, we have always had to overcome a multitude of challenges, which is the beauty of the unshakeable entrepreneurial spirit. Entrepreneurs are inherently positive thinkers and are generally optimistic, which gives us a unique ability to persevere and shine our brightest when we're in our darkest and most desperate hour. As I write this book in July 2020, I see the steely resolve and competitive spirit of so many individuals, organizations, and companies throughout the Memphis area (and the country), all putting forth an unbelievable response to this invisible enemy. And these same people are also filled with incredible resilience, compassion, boundless determination, and perseverance.

Adversity will always be with us. If your business has struggled with the COVID-19 fallout, know that as we go through adversity, we get stronger. And who knows? It may also end up being a key factor in growing the value of your business long term, which could very well make it attractive to potential acquirers.

There are so many stories of doctors, nurses, and other healthcare workers all across the country who are on the front lines, risking their lives each and every day to save others. We hear stories of random acts of kindness from so many people throughout the country who truly understand we are all in it together. Many building owners and landlords are doing all they can to help out by waiving rent for several months to support small businesses, restaurants, coffee shops, etc. Also, several Fortune 500 companies have adapted their business to help out the cause by manufacturing much-needed ventilators and hand sanitizers.

There is no question that these are incredibly challenging times that have inspired people to do incredible things on so many fronts. I do believe that COVID-19 is a moment in time and that in the coming days there will be even more inspiring moments all across our country demonstrating the resiliency, determination, and ingenuity of the American people.

Finally, when I think about the current crisis and how our country is responding to all of the challenges and uncertainty, I remember a scene from the movie *Apollo 13*. At a critical point in the mission, Flight Director Gene Kranz overhears two NASA directors discussing the low survival chances for the crippled spacecraft: "This could be the worst disaster NASA has ever experienced."

"With all due respect, sir," Kranz replies, "I believe this is going to be our finest hour."

Acknowledgments

When I first thought about writing this book, I knew it would not only be challenging but highly emotional as well. It's one thing to write about the ups and downs of starting and growing a business, like I did in my first two books (*Keep Swinging* and *Hitting the Curveballs*), but the emotional road of selling a business I created was a far more complex journey.

I have so many people to thank for encouraging me not only to tell our acquisition story but also to share the lessons I learned on my twenty-plus year journey with ISI. Your feedback has reinforced my belief that the concepts shared in this book will be useful to the many entrepreneurs and small business owners who want to know what it takes to build a business that has value and is attractive to a potential acquirer.

I want to start by thanking my wife Maureen, who really is the "wind beneath my wings," as well as my son Jordan and daughter Kaitlin, who have been on this incredible ride with me and ISI from the very beginning. My success as an entrepreneur is a tribute to the three of you, who have always provided me with unconditional love and steadfast support. Thanks for always believing in me and giving me the opportunity to chase my dream.

I want to also thank all the employees, customers, and business partners at ISI for their dedication and long-term support. Building a successful company is a group effort, and I am fortunate to have had all of you on my team for so many years. You truly are the best.

I also want to thank the rest of my family and friends for their unwavering support for all these years. It has meant the world to me. Starting, growing, and eventually selling ISI has been quite a journey, and I thank all of you for being a part of it. A special thanks to my brother-in-law Mike Wido, who recommended the title for this book. After reading my first two books, he knew this one also had to have a baseball theme. Additional thanks go out to Dr. Jeffrey Kerlan for his long-term support and for helping me come up with such a special title for the last chapter.

I want to thank my talented editor, Amanda Rooker at Split Seed Media, whose collaboration and insights from beginning to end made this work possible. You believed in me and this book from the start, and for that I will always be grateful.

I want to thank Megan Dutta and the entire team at *Systems Contractor News* (*SCN*) magazine for providing me the opportunity to be a guest columnist for such a wonderful publication. I have enjoyed writing for *SCN* these past several years and hope you like the way we reworked some of my past Viewpoint articles for this book. You folks are the best, and I will always appreciate your ongoing support.

Many thanks to David Hancock, Jim Howard, Margo Toulouse, Nickcole Watkins, Taylor Chaffer, Bethany Marshall, and the entire team at Morgan James Publishing for their outstanding support in making this book possible. I will always remember that Morgan James took a chance on me thirteen years ago and has never stopped believing in me and my writing.

Thanks to Jon Sparks, Jeffrey Goldberg, Frank Murtaugh and all my friends at Inside Memphis magazine for your long-term support and all the wonderful articles about me and ISI through the years. You made me look better than I deserve

Thanks to Dr. Kathy Tuberville, Dr. Chuck Pierce, Dr. Damon Fleming, Dr. Irvin Tankersly, Dr. Laura Alderson, Dr. Frances Fabian, Dr. Balaji Krishnan, Madan Birla, Mike Hoffmeyer, and all my friends and associates at the University of Memphis Fogelman College of Business and Economics (FCBE) and the Crews Center for Entrepreneurship. Your ongoing support of student entrepreneurship is so important in helping shape the business leaders of tomorrow.

I also want to acknowledge James Zebrowski and the whole team at the Collegiate Entrepreneurs Organization (CEO). Thank you for allowing me to be a part of such a special program. It has been my honor to work with so many students these past several years and help them chase their dreams.

Thanks to Eric, Andre, and all the good folks at Start Co. for your long-term support and for allowing me to be a part of such an exciting organization. You guys are definitely making a difference, not only in the Memphis business community but across the nation as well.

I also want to thank Pearson Crutcher, Walker Uhlhorn, Mike Bruns, Dr. Scott Morris, and all the members of the Society of Entrepreneurs for allowing me to be a part of such a prestigious organization. Being an SOE member is truly one of the highlights of my business career, and I will always appreciate the opportunity SOE affords me to help other local entrepreneurs achieve the kind of success they are striving for.

I want to thank Chip Marston, Garner Williams, Caren Creason, Leslie Entrekin, and all of our friends at the Marston Group for their help and advice in guiding us through the countless accounting and financial issues associated with the M&A process. We could not have done it without all of you, and I will always appreciate your patience and steady support when we needed it most.

Lastly, I want to thank Laurel Williams and her team at Burch Porter and Johnson, who provided us the much-needed M&A experience and professional legal advice that was so crucial in closing the biggest deal of my career. Your expertise and professionalism made the difference.

About the Author

Jay B. Myers is the current president of JBM Enterprises and past founder/CEO of Interactive Solutions Inc. (ISI), a Memphis-based firm that specializes in videoconferencing, distance learning, telemedicine, and audio-visual sales and support. Jay started ISI in 1996 and built it into a twenty-million-dollar company with fifty-five employees and offices in Memphis, Nashville, Knoxville, and Little Rock.

ISI has received numerous corporate awards and much recognition, including being named to *Inc.* magazine's list of the fastest growing private companies in the United States seven times in eleven years.

In 2007, Jay published his first book, *Keep Swinging: An Entrepreneur's Story of Overcoming Adversity and Achieving Small Business Success* and subsequently was presented the 2010 Ethan Award for success as an entrepreneurial author. Jay was inducted into the Christian Brothers High School Hall of Fame in 2011.

In 2014, Jay published his second book, *Hitting the Curveballs: How Crisis Can Strengthen and Grow Your Business*, in which he shares inspiring stories and practical tips based on growing ISI's revenue from eleven million to twenty-five million during the Great Recession (2007–2011). In 2017, ISI was named one of the Top Work Places in Memphis by the *Commercial Appeal*.

Jay was inducted into the Society of Entrepreneurs in 2018 and was recently named executive in residence at the University of Memphis Fogelman College of Business and Economics.

Jay is active in numerous community organizations in the Memphis area, having been the past chairman and a current board member/executive committee member of the Better Business Bureau of the Mid-South. Jay is a long-term supporter of the BBB and has been on the board for over seventeen years.

In November 2018, Jay sold ISI to the largest audio-visual integration firm in the world.

He and his wife Maureen live in Collierville, Tennessee, and Holmes Beach, Florida, and have two children, Jordan and Kaitlin, as well as a white Labrador named Walker.

Book Jay to Speak

As a successful small business owner, Jay is deeply committed to promoting entrepreneurship in an effort to help others chase their dreams. A natural storyteller, Jay is a sought-after speaker at CEO conferences and entrepreneurial development programs where he shares inspiring stories and practical tips based on growing ISI's revenue from eleven million to twenty-five million during the Great Recession. Jay's message reveals creative, practical strategies to achieve business success in difficult times.

Jay's third book, *Rounding Third and Heading for Home,* gives an up-close and personal look at the many components that go into the sale of your business from someone who has gone through it. Key takeaways include what to do and what not to do in the M&A process, why it is so important to sell a business when it's ready—not when you're ready—and how to know when it's ready.

As a veteran entrepreneur, Jay also shares many of the hard-earned lessons learned after twenty-plus years running a technology business, covering topics such as the importance of mentors, knowing your company brand, not burning bridges, and reinventing your business before it's too late.

From intimate settings to delivering the keynote address at your next conference, you can book Jay to speak to your group by contacting Executive Speakers Bureau at http://executivespeakers.com, or feel free to book him directly by emailing him at jay@jaymyersceo.com or by going to his website at http://jaymyersceo.com.

Endnotes

1   Mike Monroe, "Here's Why So Many Successful Entrepreneurs Got Their Start in Sales," February 19, 2018, https://www. entrepreneur.com/article/309158.

2   Steli Efti, "5 Mega-Successful Entrepreneurs Who Launched Their Careers in Sales," https://blog.close.com/5-mega-successful-entrepreneurs-who-launched-their-careers-in-sales/, accessed June 10, 2020.

3   Efti, "5 Mega-Successful Entrepreneurs Who Launched Their Careers in Sales."

4   Dave Roos, "10 Companies That Completely Reinvented Themselves," *How Stuff Works*, https://money.howstuffworks. com/10-companies-reinvented-themselves1.htm.

5   Greg Iacurci, "Job Losses Remain 'Enormous': Coronavirus Unemployment Claims Are Worst in History," CNBC.com, July 9, 2020, https://www.cnbc.com/2020/07/09/coronavirus-unemployment-benefits-claims-are-the-worst-in-history.html.

6   Andrew Soergel, "More Than Half of Small Businesses Closed Temporarily Amid Coronavirus Outbreak," *US News and World Report*, May 5, 2020, https://www.usnews.com/news/economy/articles/2020-05-05/more-than-half-of-small-businesses-closed-temporarily-amid-coronavirus-outbreak.

A free ebook edition is available with the purchase of this book.

To claim your free ebook edition:

1. Visit MorganJamesBOGO.com
2. Sign your name CLEARLY in the space
3. Complete the form and submit a photo of the entire copyright page
4. You or your friend can download the ebook to your preferred device

Print & Digital Together Forever.

| Snap a photo | Free ebook | Read anywhere |

CPSIA information can be obtained
at www.ICGtesting.com
Printed in the USA
JSHW041247010522
25467JS00002B/183